Overcoming the spirit of Jeze

OVERCOMING THE SPIRIT OF
Perversion in a generation of S

Copyright c 2015 *by Brondon Mathis*

All Rights reserved

Unless otherwise noted, all Scripture quotations are from the King James Version of the Bible. Copyright 1979, 1980, 1982 by Thomas Nelson, Inc, publishers. Used by permission.

Scripture quotations marked NIV are from the Holy Bible, New International Version. Copyright 1973, 1978, 1984, International Bible Society. Used Permission

Cover design by Brondon Mathis

ISBN-978-1515336907

Printed in the United States of America.

Dedication

To my wife Noe, the epitome of the Proverbs 31:10 virtuous woman. You are far more precious than Jewels. The longer we dwell together, the more I love you.

Table of Contents

Introduction 5

Chapter 1 - My 25 year Experience and Testimony getting free from the Spirit of Jezebel 11

Chapter 2 – The Origin and Operation of Jezebel 21

Chapter 3 - Come out of Her My People 39

Chapter 4 – Not Ashamed of the Gospel of Christ 55

Chapter 5 - Personal transformation the revelation of God's righteousness and the gospel of Grace 73

Chapter 6 - The Spirit of Elijah and Deliverance from the Principality of Jezebel over Cities 93

Chapter 7 - Overcoming Sexual Perversion by Gods Love and Laws 113

Chapter 8 – A Covenant with my Eyes and Body 125

Chapter 9 - LGBT Discrimination Gay Marriage - Civil Rights Civil Disobedience or Moral Disobedience 139

Chapter 10 - A Dream of the Coming Expression of Jezebel in the Public Square 155

Chapter 11 - A Prayer Encounter with the Glorified Christ to Overcome the Jezebel Spirit 163

Chapter 12 - The Purity Stand of Phinehas 177

Chapter 13 – The New Heart frees you from the Jezebel Spirit 189

Overcoming the spirit of Jezebel

INTRODUCTION

THE JEZEBEL SPIRIT IN OUR GENERATION

Rev 2:18 "And to the angel of the church in Thyatira write: 'The words of the Son of God, who has eyes like a flame of fire, and whose feet are like burnished bronze. 19 "I know your works, your love and faith and service and patient endurance, and that your latter works exceed the first. 20 But I have this against you, that you tolerate that woman Jezebel, who calls herself a prophetess and is teaching and seducing my servants to practice sexual immorality and to eat food sacrificed to idols. 21 I gave her time to repent, but she refuses to repent of her sexual immorality. 22. Behold, I will throw her onto a sickbed, and those who commit adultery with her I will throw into great tribulation, unless they repent of her works...29. He who has an ear, let him hear what the Spirit says to the churches. (ESV)

What is the spirit of Jezebel? Who is Jezebel and why is it important that we overcome her? What connection does this spirit have with the current moral crisis that this generation is experiencing in its emerging expression of perverted sexuality? The spirit of Jezebel is at the center of this generations attempt to liberate our nation and world from all godly expressions of human sexuality. It is actually an all-out evil, sinister agenda and ploy to mock God. Jezebel hides her agenda to mock God through perverted sexuality in terms like feminism, tolerance and marriage equality. But it's all a ploy to mock God. Liberated sexuality is how she hides perversion. It's the religion of this generation. Just drive down the strip of any major city and you will see her church buildings – strip clubs - lined up and down those blocks, several on every strip. The religion of Jezebel is the religion of sex – sex with a purpose. It is sex that defiles individuals that were made in the image of God, and it is meant to mock their creator. (1)

Without question, the spirit of Jezebel has launched an offensive against today's generation to confuse the sexuality of this age and to take down the purity of this generation, imprisoning them in lifestyles of immorality. (1 *Jezebel – The Witch is Back by Landon Schott, Famous Publishing*)

But why today? Bob Sorge, in his book, *"A Covenant with My Eyes"* says, it has to do with how natural history will end. Revelation 14:1, 4-5 bears this out, saying;

Rev 14:1 Then I looked, and behold, on Mount Zion stood the Lamb, and with him 144,000 who had his name and his Father's name written on their foreheads….4 <u>*It is these who have not defiled themselves with women, for they are virgins*</u>*. It is these who follow the Lamb wherever he goes. These have been redeemed from mankind as first fruits for God and the Lamb, 5 and in their mouth no lie was found, for they are blameless….8 Another angel, a second, followed, saying, "*<u>*Fallen, fallen is Babylon the great, she who made all nations drink the wine of the passion of her sexual immorality.*</u>

God's archenemy doesn't want this generation of consecrated virgins to arise in the earth. Why? Because their faithfulness to God in the area of their sexuality and commitment to his principles and standards of morality will contribute to the events that precipitate the return of Jesus Christ to the earth (2 Peter 3:12). The context of the return of Israel's Messiah to the earth is the spirit of Jezebel making the nations drunk off of sexual immorality. The spirit of Jezebel is directly connected to the great whore of Babylon described in Revelation 14:8, and Revelation 17:1-2, which is a system of perversion and corruption established to entrap the generation of the Lord's return in a snare of evil and darkness, inhibiting them from recognizing, desiring and accepting the Lord's Messiah and his coming Kingdom of righteousness, peace and joy in the earth. When you see this system of Babylon falling in Rev. 14:8, being directly connected to the nations being drunken off of sexual immorality, you can see the inevitable end of this generation's downward spiral into sexual perversion towards the end of the age - *a great release of God's judgment on the earth.*

How do we overcome this spirit in order to avoid the great collapse along with this great Whore of Babylon? How does the church stand against sexual immorality in the midst of a generation being deceived in their sexuality and anesthetized against immorality? We must know what we're fighting against. And we must know our weapons. The bible reveals who were fighting against, and the weapons of our warfare in Ephesians 6:12 and 2 Corinthians 10:4

Eph. 6:12 For we do not wrestle against flesh and blood, but against the rulers, against the authorities, against the cosmic powers over this present darkness, against the spiritual forces of evil in the heavenly places. 13 Therefore take up the whole armor of God, that you may be able to withstand in the evil day, and having done all, to stand firm.

2 Co 10:4 for the weapons of our warfare are not of the flesh but have divine power to destroy strongholds. 5. We destroy arguments and every lofty opinion raised against the knowledge of God, and take every thought captive to obey Christ, 6. Being ready to punish every disobedience, when your obedience is complete.

We're not fighting against the courts, Presidents, politicians or radio personalities. We're not fighting against liberals, conservatives, democrats, republicans or tea partiers. We're not fighting against homosexuals, lesbians, pornographers, adulterers, or fornicators. We're not fighting against Hollywood, the liberal media, the gay activists or their gay agenda. We're fighting against the spirit of Jezebel in all of her various forms and expressions. **And it's a spiritual battle that requires (1) a heightened spirituality, (2) divine revelation and (3) grace from God to follow the lamb (Jesus Christ) wherever he goes (Rev. 14:4).** And until we tap into that revelation and grace from God and understand Jezebels various expressions and how to recognize and resist this spirit to overcome her seductions, future generations will be caught off guard, deceived by her teachings, with the final generation being completely taken out by her, perverting and delaying the generation of the Lord's return.

2Pe 3:10 But the day of the Lord will come like a thief, and then the heavens will pass away with a roar, and the heavenly bodies will be burned up and dissolved, and the earth and the works that are done on it will be exposed. 11 Since all these things are thus to be dissolved, what sort of people ought you to be in lives of holiness and godliness. 12 waiting for and hastening the coming of the day of God...

Rev 2:20 Notwithstanding I have a few things against thee, because <u>thou suffers that woman Jezebel, which calls herself a prophetess, to teach and to seduce my servants to commit fornication</u>, and to eat things sacrificed unto idols. Rev 2:21 And I gave her space to repent of her fornication; and she repented not. 22 <u>Behold, I will cast her into a bed, and them that commit adultery with her into great tribulation, except they repent of their deeds.</u>

It's imperative that those that name the name of Christ not fall into this immoral trap and seduction from this spirit. If so, the day of the Lord's judgment will come on His Church like a thief in the night. This day is not supposed to come upon the Church as a thief. We're supposed to be the one's hastening that day, through our Love for Him and His appearing, and through our faithfulness to His Word and His ways.

One of the punishments that Revelation 2:21 lists to those that give in to this spirit of Jezebel and to her perverted teachings, is that Christ will throw Jezebel into a sickbed, and those who commit adultery with her (come into covenant with her teachings) into great tribulation, unless they repent. This is where our sexually immoral society is heading – Great Tribulation, as we acquiesce to Jezebels expressions of sexual perversion - same sex marriage, and the transgender and sex change movement, championed by Bruce Jenner. But this book is not sounding the alarm against the secular societal moral collapse of our generation, nor its sexually perverted ideology being preached by Jezebels prophets - *the media and the pop entertainment culture*. This book is sounding the alarm for believers in Christ, to come out of her perverted ideological sexuality before it's too late, before the coming Judgment of the day of the Lord. The judgments of the day of the Lord are where many that name the name "Christian" are headed if we don't learn how to come out of Jezebels expression of sexuality, overcome her, and resist her seductions, to stand against this spirit in the earth. The only way those that name the name of Christ will be able to avoid the judgments that will be released upon this age right before the return of the Christ, is to repent of her teachings, and return to Christ's expression of sexuality seen in the scripture. Revelation 17:1-5 says;

Overcoming the spirit of Jezebel

1 Then one of the seven angels who had the seven bowls came and said to me, "<u>Come, I will show you the judgment of the great prostitute who is seated on many waters</u>, 2 with whom the kings of <u>the earth have committed sexual immorality, and with the wine of whose sexual immorality the dwellers on earth have become drunk.</u>" 3 And he carried me away in the Spirit into a wilderness, and I saw a woman sitting on a scarlet beast that was full of blasphemous names, and it had seven heads and ten horns. 4 The woman was arrayed in purple and scarlet, and adorned with gold and jewels and pearls, <u>holding in her hand a golden cup full of abominations and the impurities of her sexual immorality</u>. 5 And on her forehead was written a name of mystery: "Babylon the great, mother of prostitutes and of earth's abominations."

The fall of Babylon – For All Nations are drunk off of Her Sexual Immorality

Rev 18:1 After this I saw another angel coming down from heaven, having great authority, and the earth was made bright with his glory. 2 And he called out with a mighty voice, "Fallen, fallen is Babylon the great! She has become a dwelling place for demons, a haunt for every unclean spirit, a haunt for every unclean bird, a haunt for every unclean and detestable beast. 3 <u>For all nations have drunk the wine of the passion of her sexual immorality, and the kings of the earth have committed immorality with her</u>, and the merchants of the earth have grown rich from the power of her luxurious living." 4 Then I heard another voice from heaven saying, "<u>Come out of her, my people, lest you take part in her sins, lest you share in her plagues; 5 for her sins are heaped high as heaven, and God has remembered her iniquities</u>. 6 Pay her back as she herself has paid back others, and repay her double for her deeds; mix a double portion for her in the cup she mixed.

This book is being written primarily to believers in Christ and His word, that struggle with all types of sexually Immoral behaviors, including, but not limited to, gender identity issues, to give biblical basis for overcoming this spirit in all of its facets and forms, as we come to the end of the age. The Bible is the basis for deliverance from all forms of immorality and sexual bondage. If you don't believe the bible and what it says about sexual immorality, or if you try to twist it to fit the immoral lifestyle of this generation, being taken in by this spirit of Jezebel and her seductive teachings, then the contents of this book will not help you. You will only be helped by this book you if you're willing to acknowledge the God of scripture and allow Him to transform your thinking and renew your mind through the Word of God to His purpose for godly sexuality within the context of biblical marriage.

The spirit of Jezebel is the spirit behind the expression of perverse sexuality in this generation. The spirit of Jezebel is the spirit behind gender confusion. The spirit of Jezebel is the spirit behind the LGBT and the so-called gay marriage agenda. The spirit of Jezebel is what's behind the abortion and pornographic industry's multi-billion dollar industries. But God has a solution. God has a remedy for those that want to be free and overcome this spirit in this generation.

This book will give you practical, spiritual and biblical ways to recognize, overcome and resist Jezebel in all of her forms. You will learn how to deal with her deceptive messages of tolerance, marriage equality and civil rights for gay and lesbian couples. The intent of this book is not to come across judgmental or to alienate unbelievers from biblical truth through the spirit of condemnation, but to be informative and instructive to those that truly want to overcome sexual immorality in all of its forms. I'm not writing this book to argue with those that don't believe in godly, biblical sexuality, or that are out to twist the biblical texts or narratives to support their immoral desires or lifestyles. I'm writing this book for those that recognize that the presentation of sexuality of this generation is headed progressively and speedily down the moral abyss of depravity and want to get off this increasingly broad highway. In this book, *"Overcoming the Spirit of Jezebel,"* you will learn how to overcome, once and for all, pornography, adultery, fornication, and yes, Homosexuality and Lesbianism, as a believer in Christ, and be prepared to hasten the day of the Lord and the return of the Bridegroom, Jesus Christ to be married to His bride, the Church.

CHAPTER 1

MY 25 YEAR EXPERIENCE AND TESTIMONY GETTING FREE FROM THE SPIRIT JEZEBEL

I still remember the movie I watched when I was 15 years old on our new cable station HBO. I was downstairs in our family's family room when the *Postman Always Rings Twice* came on in 1981. The sensuous wife of a lunch wagon proprietor and a ruthless drifter begin a sordidly steamy affair and conspired to murder her Greek husband. All I can remember about the movie was the steamy sex scene that left an indelible imprint on my brain. It was at this point, in my young adolescence, that I became intrigued by sex, and hooked on pornographic material. In his excellent book called Jezebel: *The Witch is Back*, Landon Schott shares how the spirit of Jezebel has gained access to a generation through a sexually charged Hollywood:

The witch is back in a sexually charged Hollywood. Movies have spread her perversions and sexuality across the world to billions of people. Pornography has made its way past magazines and onto phones. The pornography industry grosses more yearly revenue than every major sport combined – Introduction XVI

This is how the spirit of Jezebel and her whoredom's gained access into my heart to begin desecrating God's image of sexuality in my spirit. This medium of cable T.V. took my mind on a ride from the late night shows on HBO to full blatant pornography, to masturbation, onto casual one night sexual encounters with girls in college, onto prostitutes in my city's streets, all before the age of 21. By the time I was married at 29 I had so much immoral sexual baggage it almost destroyed my marriage and God's identity of my life to be a godly man, husband and father. What was even worse, was at 22 I somehow sifted through all of that immorality to hear and yield to God's call on my life to be a preacher of the Gospel. And even though I was sincere and after the heart of God, I was full of sexual immorality and bound to severe sexual addictions, mainly to strange women, that I had little contact with. This was the context that I began my adulthood, my marriage and my family. And even though I was married with babies, and in the ministry I was still bound and couldn't get free from sexual immorality. This is where many Christians that attend Church every week, find themselves, bound by the spirit of Jezebel, tangled up in their minds with all kinds of sexually immoral images and addictions that prevents them from being all God has for them to be. From the age of 15 into my 40's I went back and forth, in and out of a struggle with the spirit of Jezebel. I would sometimes go a year or two in relative freedom, only to relapse into some past immoral cycle with a past sexual addiction. It was during this time that I wondered if I would ever be free, or if freedom was even a realistic goal. I began to be satisfied with managing my sexually immoral habits, just enough to be able to function in the appearance of being morally and sexually pure, all the while there was a raging addiction down within.

It was in my 40's after over 25 years of struggling with sexual sins that I realized I needed to get some help getting free from this spirit or I was going to lose everything God had given and promised me, just like Solomon warns us in Proverbs 5-7. It wasn't until this point when I resigned ministry and moved to Kansas City to receive ministry at the International House of Prayer that I finally began to believe that I could be free, and begin setting my heart with God to pursue, once and for all, sexual purity and complete and total deliverance from the spirit of Jezebel.

Taboo deliverance vs. Biblical Full Gospel Deliverance

This type of deliverance is often not something many believe they can obtain or have, even those that believe in the power of God and prayer to break us free from the bondages of sin and evil. Often times this is because many believers misunderstand the power of God and the process of deliverance through the power of God. We misunderstand that God's process to deliverance often involves being delivered in three arenas of man's make up, spirit, soul and body. And many believers, especially spirit-filled believers, emphasize the deliverance that comes through the power of the spirit of God and often neglect the other two areas of the soul and the body (flesh), which often-times requires a more psychological, physiological approach, through the ongoing renewing of the mind through the word of God, as well as, through well-equipped, professional psychologist and-or ministers that specialize in soul deliverance through ongoing counselling (discipleship) ministry. Many Spirit-filled believers in Christendom reject this type of deliverance approach for the more sensationalized and oftentimes legitimate power of God's spirit in operation in the casting out devils. We attempt to label everything a devil. The devil is behind all vices of evil, but everything is not the devil to be cast out. While deliverance by the casting out of devils is a legitimate, biblical approach to deliverance, which Jesus operated in, this does not neglect the operation of soul deliverance through the ongoing discipleship-counseling ministry of the renewing of the mind for deliverance, which Jesus also operated in with His disciples and others. This is also, definitely a valid New Testament approach to deliverance, most commonly referred to as the renewing of the mind. (Romans 12:1-3).

This method however, is often neglected in so-called, spirit-filled Christendom, in the name of spiritual deliverance through the so-called, "power of God," as if the discipleship-counseling, psychological, physiological and soul-based renewing of the mind approach to deliverance, is not the "power of God." Below is a blog article by a Pastor, Ted Haggard, a prominent Christian minister, who's struggle with sexual sin came out to the public many years ago, while he was leading thousands weekly in Pastoral ministry. This article explains how many in the Christian Church neglect the deliverance that comes through the soul being renewed and transformed, by ongoing discipleship from professional counselling. He explains how and why many Pastors that have neglected their souls, to the emphasis of their pseudo, religious spiritual presentations, are now being defeated by the spirit of Jezebel, and committing suicide and being victimized by this ungodly neglect of soul-mental deliverance.

Suicide, Evangelicalism, and Sorrow – By Ted Haggart

Joel Hunter, pastor of Northland Church, and Rick Warren, pastor of Saddleback Church, both had sons take their own lives this year. I know of five other wonderful Christian families that also had sons who took their own lives. Some researchers are reporting that the suicide rate among Evangelicals is the same as that of the non-Christian community. How sad. Back in my NAE days, I knew Joel and Rick. They are both sincere, wonderful believers with ministries that are admired. I also knew some of the parents of the kids who took their lives here in Colorado Springs. Good families.

The news about Pastor Isaac Hunter breaks my heart. Great speaker, lover of God, and my guess is he loved the church. But he, like all of us, fell short. In the midst of divorce with accusations swirling, he resigned from the church he founded. He gave it his best shot, and his heart was broken. This makes me sick to my stomach. Don't get me wrong, I'm not sick that he fell short, that's a given for everyone except Christ Himself, I'm sick that our message did not do what we all hoped – it did not fix the problem.

In the past we would try to argue that Evangelical leaders who fall were not sincere believers, or were unrepentant, or that they did not really believe their Bibles, or were not adequately submitted. And in the midst of these arguments, we KNOW those ideas are, in some cases, rationalizations. I can offer some guesses from personal experience as well as knowledge of others' stories that, 1) Matthew Warren repeatedly prayed for God to heal his mind, and 2) Isaac Hunter frequently repented of the things in him that damaged his heart and marriage. I think Jimmy Swaggart, Jim Bakker, and I know Ted Haggard, hated their sins, repented, prayed, fasted, memorized Scripture, and pleaded with God for personal holiness. I think there are very few hypocrites in our pulpits or on church staffs. I believe most people in ministry are sincere followers of Christ. But when God's holiness is infused into our humanity that sets us all up for some degree of struggle.

I was so ashamed in 2006 when my scandal broke. The therapeutic team that dug in on me insisted that I did not have a spiritual problem or a problem with cognitive ability, and that I tested in normal ranges on all of my mental health tests (MMPI, etc.). Instead, I had a physiological problem rooted in a childhood trauma, and as a result, needed trauma resolution therapy. I had been traumatized when I was 7 years old, but when Bill Bright led me to the Lord when I was 16, I learned that I had become a new creature, a new person, and that I did not need to be concerned about anything in my past, that it was all covered by the blood. I did become a new creation spiritually, but I have since learned that I needed some simple care that would have spared my family and me a great deal of loss and pain.

Contrary to popular reports, my core issue was not sexual orientation, but trauma. I went through EMDR, a trauma resolution therapy, and received some immediate relief and, as promised, that relief was progressive. When I explain that to most Evangelical leaders, their eyes glaze over. They just don't have a grid for the complexity of it all. It is much more convenient to believe that every thought, word, and action is a reflection of our character, our spirituality, and our core. They think the Earth is flat. Everyone is either completely good or bad, everything is either white or black, and if people are sincere Christians, then they are good and their behavior should conform.

Not so. There are more grays in life than many of our modern theological positions allow. It would be easy if I were a hypocrite, Bakker was a thief, and Swaggart was a pervert. None of that is true. Because I've not communicated with the Warrens or the Hunters since late 2006, I do not know for sure, but my experience would suggest that the Warren's have received some hurtful communications from other Christians saying their son had a demon that could have been taken care of if they would have simply taken their son to them for deliverance. No doubt Isaac also received some brutal mail from Christians after his resignation from his church. My sin never made me suicidal, but widespread church reaction to me did.

I can only imagine what many Christians must go through trying to reconcile the things we Evangelicals say are true with the realities of their own lives. Do we actually believe that the many pastors who have been characterized as fallen decided to be hateful, immoral, greedy, or deceitful? I think not.

In my case, I was taught that life transformation took place at salvation and the power to overcome was inherent with the baptism in the Holy Spirit. My early Christian training was given by those who did not respect the mental health profession, nor the field of neural science. So I believed the solution to my struggle was exclusively spiritual, which turned out to be counterproductive.

If I prayed and fasted, I was more tempted. If I just worked in ministry, I experienced relief and was not tempted. I thought it was spiritual warfare. It was not. My struggle was easily explained by a competent therapeutic team.

But many in the church-world had to demonize the facts. My accuser failed his lie detector test and refused to take another, and I passed four lie detector tests given by three different polygraphers saying that the primary accusations were false. This so confused the narrative the church wanted to publicly present, they hid the tests from the public. The lead overseer actually told me, "Brother Ted, we do not believe in this psychological mumbo-jumbo, but we need to send you to therapy for the sake of the public. Then when you get home, we'll get this demon out of you and your family and sweet Miss Gayle will be just fine." I thank God for the therapy. It answered 30 years of prayer. I became the man I had always prayed to be because of the process I went through during the crisis. Though I do believe there is a need for deliverance in some situations, for that sincere overseer, the world is way too flat.

Saints, I have a high view of Scripture and am persuaded that the theological underpinnings of Evangelicalism are valid, but I am growing away from the Evangelical culture we have created. I think our movement has abandoned the application of the Gospel, and as a result we spend too much time on image management and damage control. Maybe we should be willing to admit that we are all growing in grace, be willing to be numbered with the transgressors, and stop over-stating and over-promising. Jesus has been faithful to all of us in the midst of our pain, our suffering, and our disappointments. Why don't we tell that? Every one of us have had sin horribly intrude in our lives after being saved and filled with the Holy Spirit, and God is faithfully healing us or has healed us. Why don't we tell that? He has never left us or forsaken us when we've said and done the wrong thing. Why don't we tell that? And when our children disappoint and hurt us, or we disappoint and hurt them, God sees us . . . and them. Why don't we tell that as well?

My heart physically hurts for the Warrens, the Hunters, and the five families that lost their sons. The pain is incredible. I don't know that it will ever heal this side of Heaven. I also hurt for Pastor Zachery Tims who died alone in a Times Square hotel room trying to get some relief, and for Pastor Cedric Cuthbert who was accused of watching child porn at work, and for Pastor David Loveless who was let go after his affair was revealed. Shall I go on? I do not believe we have a problem because these and so many others are insincere or because we have not adequately emphasized holiness. I think we have a core, fundamental, essential problem with our application of the Gospel. We need to re-read the New Testament and modify some of our interpretations. The Bible is true. God is faithful. But at this point, too many are missing the mark.

I know this is too long, and I would like to stop, but I can't . . . not until I say one more thing. Everyone I've mentioned here has fallen because of obvious sin. But I did not mention the proud, envious, gluttonous, angry, greedy, blamers and scrutinizers in the body of Christ who have equally fallen but their sins are acceptable in our culture so they do not even realize their sin or need for repentance. Why? They are too busy with the sins of others. Often we actually laude these Pharisees and Judaizers because of their stand against sin, not realizing that they are still not teaching us the New Testament solution to mankind's sin problem. When the New Testament becomes Torah in their hands, that law, too, stimulates sin.

It's time for us to stop what we're doing and weep. We need to repent, enter into the prayer closet without cameras, notes, or any announcements that we're praying and fasting, and repent for what we have created until our hearts are soft again. Our children are dying. Our relationships are broken. Our attitudes are arrogant. And our hearts are left confused.

This Was What I Had To Come To Grips With

This was what I had to come to grips with, well into my middle ages, beginning at 40 years old, when I made the conscience decision to untangle the strongholds of the spirit of Jezebel in my life that was manifesting herself in perverse sexual sins, that had gotten an entry way into my mind and flesh, back in my childhood. At this level of deliverance there are in-depth ongoing processes that have to be administered to you, from those that are well-equipped in ministering to your soul, to break you free from these strongholds that are deeply lodged in who you have become as an adult. Often times they're unrecognizable on the surface because many are not aware that they originated, not just from spiritual forces from the womb, but from our ungodly mindsets and ideologies that we're operating in, from the spirit of this age, which is the spirit of Jezebel, that's in the world, that appears to be normal or accepted ways of operating, thinking and functioning in life. If these strongholds are deeply rooted in a lifestyle or mindset of operating that we have bought into, deep within the make-up of who we are, we could be plagued with an impenetrable behavioral vice, habit, lifestyle, completely diametrically opposed to how God originally created us to live, which is in covenant with the spirit of the age, or the spirit of Jezebel, lodged deep within your soul. To get free you will have to first COME OUT OF HER – the spirit of this age, and of Jezebel (Revelation 18:4), and return to *the Spirit of the LORD, - the Spirit of wisdom and understanding, the spirit of counsel and of might, the spirit of knowledge and of the spirit of the fear of the Lord* (Isaiah 11:1-4).

In our society today the culture of this generation has completely and totally bought into the Jezebelian agenda and lifestyle of perverted sexuality, including same sex attraction of homosexuality and lesbianism as an accepted sexual orientation. This ungodly mindset and ideology has been pushed off on the culture of this generation in very intentional and purposeful ways, beginning now in public education in grade school. The only way to come out and stay clear of this Jezebelian spirit in this generation is to come out of the system, meaning all the institutions of public education, including most of our 21st century expressions of institutional religion, as well as the influence of the entertainment, arts and media industry, and get involved in the process of reforming these institutions through the spirit of God's wisdom and through getting involved in institutional reform of our governmental, political process. Yes, we must get involved. We must not come out to detach, but to take over and lead a generation back to God. The two areas of institutional religion and the influence of the entertainment and media industry, along with the legislative, judicial and executive branches of government, are the main bastions in Jezebels fight for the minds of a generation. Until we come out of these expressions in society and become spiritually and financially independently wealthy enough to establish our own biblically-based educational system, own the media TV/Movie studios of our day, to relay our biblically based ideology, and until we're able to raise up lobbying groups like the gay agenda, with enough monies to influence the establishment of biblically based laws in society, we will be subject to the spirit of Jezebel and her perverse presentation of spiritual and sexual or entation. In this book we will see how through scripturally based, spiritual renewal of our minds and through deliverance from the ungodly systems of Jezebel which will be exposed in this book, we can be delivered from her perverted expressions of spirituality and sexuality in the generation of the Lord's return.

CHAPTER 2

THE ORIGIN AND OPERATION OF JEZEBEL

Gen 3:1. *Now the serpent was more crafty than any other beast of the field that the LORD God had made. He said to the woman, "Did God actually say, 'You shall not eat of any tree in the garden'?"*

The woman Jezebel was an Old Testament personality that was the daughter of a pagan King, Ethbaal, King of the Sidonians, which married King Ahab, king of the nation of Israel, and influenced Israel from the worship of Jehovah to the worship of Baal, the god of the Sidonians. This woman, Jezebel is mentioned both in the Old Testament and New Testament. Jezebel in the Old Testament and Jezebel in the New Testament were two completely different ladies, but they operated in the same spirit - *the spirit of perversion and sorcery*. Her spirit was exhilarated by perversion, position, and power or prestige. When we refer to the power of Jezebel, we're not just talking about Jezebel having a control spirit. We're talking about encountering a transcendent dimension in the demonic realm. That is what these Jezebels were about in both the Old Testament and the New Testament. Here is what the Old Testament Jezebel did:

1Ki 16:31 *And it came to pass, as if it had been a light thing for him to walk in the sins of Jeroboam the son of Nebat,* **that he (Ahab) took to wife Jezebel the daughter of Ethbaal king of the Zidonians, and went and served Baal, and worshipped him. 32 And he reared up an altar for Baal in the house of Baal, which he had built in Samaria.** *33 And Ahab made a grove; and Ahab did more to provoke the LORD God of Israel to anger than all the kings of Israel that were before him.*

1Ki 19:1 *And Ahab told Jezebel all that Elijah had done, and withal how he had slain all the prophets (of Baal) with the sword. 2 Then Jezebel sent a messenger unto Elijah, saying, So let the gods do to me, and more also, if I make not thy life as the life of one of them by tomorrow about this time.*

Was it not told my lord what I did <u>when Jezebel slew the prophets of the LORD</u>, how I hid an hundred men of the LORD'S prophets by fifty in a cave, and fed them with bread and water? (1Ki 18:13)

Jezebel hated Elijah, the prophet of Israel, and wanted to kill all the prophets of Jehovah and set up her prophets of Baal as the spiritual voice and word over Israel. The New Testament Jezebel sought to kill the prophets too, but by dulling their spirits through sexual perversion, pornography and immorality. She is not killing them with a sword like the Old Testament Jezebel.

Rev 2:20 *Notwithstanding I have a few things against thee,* <u>***because you allow that woman Jezebel, which calls herself a prophetess, to teach and to seduce my servants to commit fornication,***</u> *and to eat things sacrificed unto idols. 21 And I gave her space to repent of her fornication; and she repented not.*

The New Testament Jezebel kills them by dulling their spirits and defiling their conscience to believe whatever perverted sexual preference you desired was okay, as long as you were happy. This New Testament woman, Jezebel, was an actual lady. She is not just a symbolic figure. Was her name actually Jezebel? I don't know. You cannot know for sure. But they all knew who she was. And the name she was operating under depicted clearly the spirit in which she was moving. It is a spirit of immorality and a spirit of sorcery. Beyond this actual woman Jezebel, was the spirit of Jezebel, which is still in the earth today, and was even in the earth before the woman Jezebel came on the scene in the Old Testament.

The Jezebel Spirit – The Spirit of Perversion

The Jezebel Spirit is a ruling spirit in the earth set against the spirit of God, the will of God and the purposes of God for mankind in the earth. The Jezebel spirit is a spirit that sets out to pervert the image of God in humanity and replace this image with an image of less than what God originally created for man. It's a spirit of perversion, which operates through sorcery to influence humanity away from God and His image for the purpose of human sexuality of a man to a woman and for the overall purpose for mankind.

The Trinity of Evil over the Masses – Leviathan, Jezebel, Python

The Jezebel spirit is one of three ruling principalities that rules over the masses in the earth, to keep the people of God that were bought with the price of the blood of Christ, from coming together, from hearing from God, speaking for God and from worshipping God. The other principalities that work alongside of the Jezebel spirit are the Leviathan Spirit (Job 41:33) and the Python Spirit (Acts 16). These three ruling principalities work as a trinity of evil in an ungodly godhead to operate as the gods of this world system. Again, these three ruling principalities that work together as an unholy trinity are; *the Spirit of Leviathan, the Spirit of Jezebel, and the Spirit of Python.*

The Leviathan Spirit - Pride

The Spirit of Leviathan in this unholy trinity represents or mirrors the Father, God in the heavenly trinity of the Godhead – *Father, Son and Holy Ghost.* The scripture says, Leviathan is the king of all those that are proud (Pride) (Job 41:33, 34).

Job 41:1 **Can you draw out leviathan** *with an hook? Or his tongue with a cord which you let down? 33 Upon earth there is not his like, who is made without fear. 34 He beholds all high things:* **he is a king over all the children of pride.**

The Spirit of Leviathan operates through humanity as mankind places himself and his word over the word of God. It's the spirit of pride that causes man to be haughty, high-minded and puffed up, not wanting God or His ways to be their guide, or to reign over them. It's interesting that the title and mantra of the whole gay and lesbian movement is GAY PRIDE, and the gay pride parades that go on all over the nation and world. Gay pride is a direct assault against God, His rule in the earth, and his image and purpose to lead humanity into the purpose of human sexuality and love in the earth.

As Father God in the heavenly trinity of the Godhead has a Son, Leviathan (*The spirit of pride*) in this trinity has a daughter (not a son), and that daughter is the *spirit of Jezebel.* The Jezebel Spirit is set up in this unholy trinity to mirror the Son of God, and she opposes the prophets, the voice of God or the Word of God (*which is why she attempts to kill the prophets with her sexual idolatry and manipulation through fear, control and disobedience, which leads to rebellion to Gods word and will*).

The Python Spirit - Divination

The third ruling spirit in the earth is the spirit of python, which is set in this unholy trinity as the spirit that mirrors and opposes the Holy Spirit and Worship to God in spirit and truth.

Act 16:16 **_And it came to pass, as we went to prayer, a certain damsel possessed with a spirit of divination (python) met us_**, *which brought her masters much gain by soothsaying: 17 The same followed Paul and us, and cried, saying, These men are the servants of the most high God, which shew unto us the way of salvation. 18 And this did she many days.* **_But Paul, being grieved, turned and said to the spirit, I command thee in the name of Jesus Christ to come out of her. And he came out the same hour._**

The Spirit of Python restricts and constricts worship in spirit and truth (John 4:24), and sets her perverted religion up as the worship that is acceptable to God, a false religion of tolerance of all of her gods and perversions of God and love in the name of God. Python restricts true worship while releasing perverted worship.

The spirit of Leviathan is the spirit of Pride, the spirit of Jezebel is the spirit of perversion, sexual Immorality and Idolatry, along with false prophetic ideologies. The spirit of Python is the spirit of false religion, worship, witchcraft or divination and sorcery. This book is focused particularly on recognizing and overcoming the Spirit of Jezebel. However, to find out more about the Spirit of Leviathan, and how to recognize and get free from that spirit of pride that keeps people groups and races divided and at odds with one another, you can find more information in my book on *"Building Cities of Refuge,"* on amazon.com.

The Operation of Jezebel

Jezebel works to shut the mouth of the prophets, or the Sons of God, by seducing and killing them off and raising up her false prophets through seducing teachings that enable sexual immorality, which is the essence of the expression of her worship to the idol gods of Baal.

*Was it not told my lord what I did <u>when Jezebel slew the prophets of the LORD</u>, how I hid an hundred men of the LORD'S prophets by fifty in a cave, and fed them with bread and water? (*1Ki 18:13*)*

Notwithstanding I have a few things against thee, because thou suffers that <u>woman Jezebel, which calls herself a prophetess, to teach and to seduce my servants to commit fornication, and to eat things sacrificed unto idols. (Rev. 2:20)</u>

The Jezebel spirit manifests through sexual immorality and witchcraft (idolatry). She seduces the prophets of God into immorality with her false teaching to disqualify them from speaking for God, then she attempts to replace them with her prophets, or her messengers of fear, manipulation and control, to worship the god of this world – Satan.

The Expression and Presentation of Jezebel

The way she expresses herself is through counterfeit authority. She attempts to attach herself to true authority and work alongside of true authority, working her whoredoms and her witchcrafts (2 Kings 9:22) to seduce and wrest that authority away from those she has aligned and intertwined with. She is often difficult to detect because she operates alongside and in step and sync with true authority in political government or in religious hierarchy. She speaks through and often times speaks for true authority, representing them as their ambassador. In other words, as with King Ahab, in I Kings 18:20, she often intermarries with God's authority and speaks for and represents the word of the King, (leaders) with her false, manipulative teaching, set to seduce and manipulate God's true and authentic word and will in the earth. Therefore, when a Jezebel spirit has gotten a stronghold in a region, she has come through the authentic voices of the land and eventually replaces their voices, that were speaking the will and word of

God (or the King) with her words, teaching her will in that region, as was the case with King Ahab in I Kings 16-18, and as is the case with many nations and heads of state throughout the nations.

Once she gets in authority she looks to cut off, or kill the voice of the Lord, or the voice of the prophets of God, as well as restrict and limit the authority of the King, or heads of state, as she did in I Kings 16-18:23. She accomplishes this all through seduction and perverse sexual immoral presentations, bringing those in control in true authority under her spell and control. She looks to accomplish this through favors and immoral, sexual offers, shrouded in worldly presentations of love (which is actually lust). This is how she presents herself to seduce the authority figures of God or of the land.

The Tree of Knowledge of Good and Evil and the Jezebel Spirit

When Jezebel presents herself, she does so as someone or something that's desirable and good or pleasant to the eyes, as it was said of the tree of the knowledge of good and evil in Genesis 3:6. The woman saw that the tree was good for food, and that it was pleasant to the eyes, and a tree to be desired, to make one wise, and she took of the fruit thereof, and did eat, and gave also unto her husband (Genesis 3:6).

This is how the Jezebel spirit gets in with true authority. She doesn't come as something evil and ugly or something undesirable to be resisted. She comes as something good and something desirable that's needed to live. But in the end she will manifest her true nature of evil and have you attracted and addicted to something totally illegitimate. Jezebel's good presentations are presented as the tree of knowledge of good and evil was presented to Eve in Genesis 3 – with good things hiding the evil ends. The only way you can resist her is through the word of God and through a continual ongoing relationship and fellowship with the will of the father and true authentic authority, to know His will. Resisting her also requires being in right relationship with others in right authority that are in a continual ongoing relationship with you and the will and Word of the father, God.

The Spouses Purpose: Given to help resist the Jezebel Spirit

Remember, after the Lord made man and put him in the garden to dress it and keep it in Genesis 2:15-17, the Lord God commanded the man, saying, *of every tree of the garden you may eat freely; But of the tree of the knowledge of Good and Evil, thou shalt not eat of it; For in the day that thou shall eat of it you shall surely die.* Immediately after that command, in Genesis 2:18, he says: IT IS NOT GOOD THAT THE MAN SHOULD BE ALONE; I WILL MAKE HIM A HELPER FIT FOR HIM. God made man a helper fit - the Woman - to help him resist the Spirit of Jezebel, which is the spirit of good and evil. Therefore in dealing with the Jezebel Spirit, it's not good for Man to be alone in what God has called him to do. This spirit comes to you as something good and desirable, and if you don't have a helper fit for you, to be in agreement with what God has told you, and to help you stay on task, you could open yourself up for the spirit of Jezebel to seduce you away from God's commands, vision and purpose for your life. She often seduces you through someone that has become close to you that is not fit for you, mainly because they are not as aware as you are of what the commands, mission or tasks of God is for your life.

Jezebel will try to get close to you, not to hear what your mission or will of God for your life is, but to fulfil bring her will to pass, or to eventually bring her will into your purpose and legitimate calling, to dilute it, compromise it and ultimately stop it. Once you give into her whoredoms and sorceries she will begin to give you a whole different way of looking at what God called you to be or told you to do. She will twist the word of the Lord, she will begin teaching you with her perverted knowledge and revelation that's not from God and will cause you to change what God said or what God created you to be or told you to do, until it's no longer God's word, but her word.

Once it's her word and not God's, or the word or constitution of the land, you can no longer recognize it, or understand it, to accomplish it and follow it. And because you no longer recognize it, you no longer have the clarity and confidence to lead and continue in what God told you to do. So you now have to look to her to lead you, and for her to direct your vision from God, with her carnal, fleshly, sense knowledge, with both GOOD AND EVIL. This is what happened to Adam. Jezebel came through Eve. Jezebel was not Eve. Eve was Adam's helpmeet to help him resist Jezebel, but because Adam didn't stay in right relationship with Eve, to continue sharing with her the vision, and because neither of them, Adam nor Eve, stayed in right relationship with God, Jezebel, through the serpent deceiving Eve, got to Adam. She came through the one closes to him, deceiving Eve with something both good and desirable. How was Eve deceived? Because Adam wasn't properly covering her, communicating the commandment of Genesis 2:16…..*And the Lord God COMMANDED THE MAN SAYING…..*

Because Adam didn't cover her with the commands of the Lord, the Jezebel spirit deceived Eve and began to work through her to change what God said, for the purpose of thwarting and stopping the will of God, for Satan's will.

Who Can Find a Virtuous Wife?

The godly expression of the Virtuous wife of Proverbs 31 is actually what covers and keeps a man from the spirit of Jezebel. In these verses we can see how a virtuous wife helps guard against the attack of Jezebel's perversion and distortion of God's will and purposes for mankind.

Pro 31:10 An excellent (virtuous) wife who can find? She is far more precious than jewels. 11 The heart of her husband trusts in her, and he will have no lack of gain.

This chapter of Proverbs actually begins with a Kings mother warning and training her son, from childhood, in preparation to become king, of how to resist and overcome the spirit of Jezebel.

Pro 31:1. The words of King Lemuel. An oracle that his mother taught him: 2. what are you doing, my son? What are you doing, son of my womb? What are you doing, son of my vows? 3 Do not give your strength to women, your ways to those who destroy kings.

These verses reveal that King Lemuel was writing an oracle that his mother taught him about how to resist the Jezebel spirit or how to resist a woman that is being manipulated by the spirit of Jezebel, to bring kings to destruction. This suggests that mothers play an important role in assisting sons in avoiding the Jezebel spirit. If a boy has not had this training concerning how to avoid Jezebel, and have not been raised at an early age to resist ungodly sexual presentations, or they have not had the right image or example from mothers, of what a godly woman looks like or how to avoid the ungodly presentation of a woman that has been deceived and manipulated by Jezebel, that boy will not be able to resist or overcome the Jezebel spirit, and that spirit will overwhelm his strength and destroy his destiny as a king in dominion in the earth. Kings that give in to Jezebels give their strength to women that will destroy them and their house. Ask King Ahab in 2Kings 9.

2Ki 9:6 So he arose and went into the house. And the young man poured the oil on his head, saying to him, "<u>Thus says the LORD, the God of Israel, I anoint you king over the people of the LORD, over Israel.</u>

<u>7 And you shall strike down the house of Ahab your master, so that I may avenge on Jezebel the blood of my servants the prophets</u>, and the blood of all the servants of the LORD.

<u>8 For the whole house of Ahab shall perish, and I will cut off from Ahab every male, bond or free, in Israel.</u> 9 And I will make the house of Ahab like the house of Jeroboam the son of Nebat, and like the house of Baasha the son of Ahijah.

Mothers must teach sons the value of virtuous wives in marital relationships, what they look like, what their function is in building a resistance against the Jezebel spirit. Proverbs 31 is King Lemuel's mother's teaching the revelation on the wife that will help godly kings overcome Jezebel. Satan knows that we are all called to be kings and priests in the earth, having dominion over the whole earth, and that if he can distort that image and pervert that expression he can keep man from exerting his dominion over planet earth, and from dispelling him and his demons from the earth.

1Pe 2:9 But you are a chosen race, a royal priesthood, a holy nation, a people for his own possession, that you may proclaim the excellencies of him who called you out of darkness into his marvelous light.

Mothers should teach by example and in word, how to recognize a virtuous wife and how to overcome the Jezebel spirit, keeping their sons from giving their strength to women that are not our wives, or to strange women that will destroy their destinies. However, when kings find a virtuous wife, King Lemuel's mother says, the heart of her husband will trust in her. The word "trust" is the Hebrew word baw-takh' which means; *to hie for refuge; figuratively to trust, be confident or sure: - be bold (confident, secure, sure), careless (one, woman)*

Pro 31:11 *The heart of <u>her husband doth safely trust in her</u>, so that he shall have no need of spoil. 12 <u>She will do him good and not evil</u> all the days of her life.*

Notice that the virtuous wife does her husband GOOD AND NOT EVIL. She does not operate in good AND evil. But Jezebel operates in both good and evil, just like the tree Satan deceived Eve to partake of. When a man or a woman chooses to use seduction and sexuality to deceive, manipulate and control an individual, a people group, or the masses, he or she has chosen to eat from the tree of knowledge of good and evil, and has given in to the spirit of Jezebel.

This, in essence, is the operation and the process of the spirit of Jezebel. Once this spirit gets in and begins operating its plan and system of good and evil, it's difficult to break free from her manacles and system of perversion, manipulation, fear, domination and control. But there is a way to overcome her. You have to COME OUT OF HER, out of her system, off of a dependency upon her ways, strategies and system. Revelation 18:4 - *And I heard another voice from heaven, saying, Come out of her, my people, that ye be not partakers of her sins, and that ye receive not of her plagues.*

Jezebels Operation through Perverted Sexuality and Immorality

The operation of the spirit of Jezebel manifests itself through the spirit of sexual perversion and immorality that manipulates and controls a generation away from God's expression and idea for intimacy and love for God and for our neighbor (spouse, family, loved ones, friends and humanity as a whole).

Mar 12:30 And thou shalt love the Lord thy God with all thy heart, and with all thy soul, and with all thy mind, and with all thy strength: this is the first commandment.

Mar 12:31 And the second is like, namely this, Thou shalt love thy neighbour as thyself. There is none other commandment greater than these.

A lot of people in Christendom, when they think about Jezebel, they think of a woman with a strong personality. If her leadership is stronger than yours and you are a man, she is a Jezebel. But the core meaning of a Jezebel spirit is a spirit of perversion and seduction that operates through witchcraft – *manipulation, deception, domination and control.* The people most engaged in and taken in by the spirit of Jezebel are men. They are the ones mainly who are producing and promoting perverted sexuality and releasing it to the masses, like pornography. They are promoting it, and they are partaking of it even more than women are. The Adult Film agency is being run by-in-large by men, although a woman now has the top Adult Film agency in the world, men are the dominate purveyors of Adult Films and pornography. The most powerful Jezebel institution in the earth is Hollywood, California—the spirit of Jezebel, pumping volumes of filth into the nations of the earth. There is, no doubt, a couple of other centers like Hollywood. But when you think Jezebel, do not think of a woman with a strong personality. Maybe the woman being accused of being a Jezebel, may need a little bit of relationship skills or she just needs a little help on this and that. But that does not make her a Jezebel. I care about this a lot because I have watched over the years, a lot of woman getting written off as having a Jezebel spirit because their personality is strong. Again, they just need to get a few rough edges smoothed out, as well as their personality skills refined. A lot of guys have the same problem and nobody says "Jezebel" to them. We are missing the whole thing because this is not the essence of what the spirit of Jezebel even is.

The Church in America

The spirit of Jezebel is alive and well in the church in America. Again, the group that is most responsible for Jezebel is mostly men. Men are the ones that are financing the pornography industry and the whole industry of immorality. It is being financed by men, promoted by men, and is partaken of by men. And women are involved in it as well, obviously. I want us to get a real grip on what Jesus is saying so that we do not marginalize the weightiness and seriousness of what He is saying to the church. I look at the church in America and I just have one huge statement about it. There is a Jezebel spirit from coast to coast, all through the church. It is a spirit of toleration with immorality. This is bad, but the warnings that Jesus gives the spirit of Jezebel are really serious. He says to the church that has this spirit on them, which is to me, the vast majority of the body of Christ in the western world, "I will send judgment to you and I will wake you up because I love you that much."

Correction for Compromise

Verse 20: "*Nevertheless I have a few things against you, because you allow that woman Jezebel who calls herself a prophetess, to teach and seduce my servants to commit sexual immorality and to eat things sacrificed to idols.*" Verse 24 (paraphrased): "*I say to you and to the rest in Thyatira, as many as do not have this doctrine, who have not known the depths of Satan, I will put on you no other burden.*" He goes on and gives a message to them.

Verse 20: "*A few things I have against you.*" It is important to know that Jesus gives one of the strongest affirmations—a five-fold affirmation—to this church, but He still has things that trouble His heart against that church. As long as Jesus is still talking to us, we have a hope and a good future. His correction is not rejection. He is talking, He is talking through His Word. That is how it starts. He speaks to our conscience. It's as if the Lord says, "Do it my way. Do it my way." We say, "OK." But we do not follow through. He says, "Do it my way. I tell you, if my Word will discipline your conscience, it is done and it is finished." "I am trying to, but I do not want to." He says, "OK, I will allow some frustrations to happen to get your attention." So the frustrations mount up. Not that all frustrations are in this category. I do not want to join Job's friendship group, his home group, those three guys who thought everything Job did was related to sin— I do not want to be in that home group. They thought everybody's trouble was related to their sin. That is not true at all. There are many troubles that are just the direct attack of the devil.

However, the Lord will allow frustrations to get our attention because of continued compromise. Then the guy says, "No, I am going to keep going." The Lord says, "OK, now I am going to really get your attention. I am going to expose you openly." The thing is building to more than a frustration. They keep going. It's as if the Lord says, "OK, I am going to allow your body to be touched in a way that is really going to get your attention because I do not want to talk to you this way, when we stand face to face in eternity. Then you would really be in trouble. I will take you at any level that you will agree. We will end the trouble there."

The force and the weightiness with which Jesus speaks to us increases in its weightiness season by season. As long as He is talking to us, we have a hope of a great future. It is when He does not talk anymore, that we are in big trouble. He says, "OK, you know what, you just stay in that affair. You just stay there." One, two, three, four years and you have not felt the conviction of the Holy Spirit. That is really troubling. You are in the final stages of trouble. However, if you are wrestling, you are sick and in pain, you are getting blocked, and the Lord is allowing circumstances to frustrate you. He is giving you dreams and even touching you in a way that you really feel the weight and the pain of it. He is saying, "I am for you. I am chasing you down. We still have a great plan ahead. You still have a lot of things that you and I can do together. If I quit doing this, you are in big trouble. Sometimes some of the big ministries get exposed and we think, "Oh how tragic." It would be far more tragic if they did not get exposed and the Lord says, "No, go do it. I will leave you alone. I will even let your ministry continue grow." That is really, really, really bad from the heavenly perspective.

Idolatry

He says, *"You allowed that woman Jezebel to teach and seduce my servants to commit sexual immorality and eat things sacrificed to idols"* (Rev.2:20). There are two things here. Right now, we are not that focused on the idolized side of the Jezebel spirit. The idol thing is going to emerge in the earth. The spirit of Jezebel is the spirit of immorality in the physical realm, and idolatry, which is to actually interact with demons. It is the quest for the transcendent. We look around in the western world and think, "Idols? How can they bow before that stone and talk to it. That seems so dumb." Well, it was not exactly like that.

Demons really appeared and made things happen. They appeared as angels. Spirit beings would appear and power would be released.

There is such a quest for the spirit to be exhilarated with power, which one of the major strongholds worldwide before the Lord returns will be, that the westerners will be buying into idolatry and sorcery. It will look different and be far more sophisticated, but it will be dynamic interaction with the spirit realm. That is what idolatry is. That is what Jezebel was into. Interaction in the spirit realm out of the will of God and interaction in the sexual realm out of the will of God. Those were the two things. Interaction in the spirit realm, we can see it mounting, but it is not at the level yet that it is going to be.

Satan's Two-Fold Strategy

The first line of attack on a global level is to weaken the morals of the planet with immorality. Then the idolatry—the demon encounters—will increase and you can be sure that in the vast majority of these demon encounters, Satan will appear as an angel of light. They will think, "That was awesome, that really worked." The immorality will set up the situation. The touching of the body in immorality will open the door for people to long for their spirit to be exhilarated in illegal ways. Bringing the two together will bring them into depths of darkness that we cannot fully grasp. That is the two-fold strategy of Satan: to bring this longing for transcendence and to allow the spirit realm—the realm of demons—to mix with the realm of immorality, through drugs, through mind altering substances, whether it is alcohol or higher level drugs—mind altering substances—so that immorality and sorcery have a far greater convergence together in the human experience. That, in a paragraph, is the spirit of Jezebel. I see this mounting up fiercely in our nation right now. I mean, the sorcery thing, we see whispers and it is growing. But the immorality, the other thing, is growing so rapidly.

Pornography

One of the main operations of the spirit of Jezebel in our nation is pornography. Again, the ones who are most responsible are the ones that are producing it and promoting it, yes, and also those who are partaking of it and obviously very seriously involved. When I think of these billionaire guys, whoever they are in the earth, they are going to stand before God one day and give an answer for how they have corrupted an entire generation. This immorality will open the door straight into the realm of the spirit. When a person's morals are reduced and their conscience is defiled, and their conscience is seared, the door into the spirit realm is far easier to get through. That is the point. That is the great point of the immorality surge from hell. The point is not that the enemy is just trying to get us distracted. He wants our spirits dulled, our consciences seared, so that we easily step over the line. I am saying that multitudes in the church will easily step over the line into the spirit realm, into the dark realm of the spirit. Their spirits will be exhilarated through mind altering substances and they will be so accustomed to and so comfortable with immorality at that time. There is only one answer, the end-time prayer movement under the leadership of Jesus and the power of God breaking in. The eyes of fire are the other expression of it.

The Woman Jezebel

This woman, Jezebel, was an actual lady. She is not just a symbolic figure. Was her name actually Jezebel? I don't know. You cannot know for sure. But they all knew who she was. And the name she was operating under depicted clearly the spirit in which she was moving. It is a spirit of immorality and it is a spirit of sorcery. I do not want us to lose sight of this and reduce this to a control spirit. Sorcery is far more than that. I am talking about a high level encounter with demon spirits. If it is a control spirit, we reduce it to a person who has a personality that bugs us. Then that is what Jezebel is and we are off the hook. Beloved, this thing is staring right down at the body of Christ, straight across America. This thing is so huge. We are all being confronted with it. Not just people who are a little pushy in their personalities. This is real and this is big. The Lord is serious about confronting it.

Saving a Nation

When I hear the voices in America—they do exist by the glory of God, but they almost do not exist. Is anybody crying out against this in the land? Will you? There are a few that we know of. However, God has His men and women all over America. It is thousands, but we need millions.

We don't have millions who are crying out in the body of Christ but thousands are. I don't want to minimize the beauty of that. What I want to do is stir us up. The sin was that they tolerated her or they allowed her teaching. One translation says tolerated, another says allowed. "You allow her to go uncontested." "Our church is not into that kind of stuff." You cannot be into Jesus and be silent on this subject. I am not talking about an angry spirit, because you have been wounded somewhere. Everybody has been wounded by somebody bringing pain to the life of a family, related to some expression of immorality. It is not enough to just be wounded by somebody near you who engaged in immorality, so you are mad at it and lashing out. That is not going to solve the problem. We are talking about a tender, clear, bold, anointed voice against this spirit. Because it will save the people, and not just get something off of our chests. It is saving a nation. I look at so many people who are wrecking their lives with immorality. The Lord wants us to feel tenderness towards them, even though they have caused a lot of pain. Not figuring out how we can pound them, but figuring out a way for them to make sense of their life in the grace of God.

Out of that spirit, we have to reach into the bridal paradigm. Looking through the lens of the bride of Christ and talking about a God who desires them. We need to tell them, that they have not gone too far. They do not need to give up and give in. God is waiting right now. All they need to do is agree with Him and they will get a brand new start. Even these top pornography guys.

Salvation of the Lost

In some of our prayer meetings, one of the things we must pray for regularly is human trafficking. I have a passion for this. I want to see these evil men, who have these women trapped in cages in basements, these evil men with demons, get so gloriously converted, that they become apostles, who are filled with tears because they love Him. The power of God is on them and they transform a nation. When we are reaching for these guys who are steeped in iniquity, they might be the next apostle. That gal might be the next apostle or prophetess; you just don't know who she is. "Yeah, but she is such a witch." "I know, but that is not bigger than the grace of God. What if she is a great prophetess a moment away? Let's go after her and see what the Lord will give us."

My point is that we are not writing them off. I am talking about the silence of the church. On the other hand, what we do not want to do is go in the other direction and say, "We are all going to be vocal," but we are angry in being vocal. No, it is the cry for the soul of a nation. It is the cry for the soul of an individual, and the church in a generation. That is what we are fighting for and we are doing it as people who have received outrageous forgiveness. We do not forget what the score is in our life which nobody knows. We cannot forget that.

CHAPTER 3

COME OUT OF HER, MY PEOPLE

Rev. 18:4 Then I heard another voice from heaven saying, <u>"Come out of her, my people, lest you take part in her sins, lest you share in her plagues;</u> 5 for her sins are heaped high as heaven, and God has remembered her iniquities

Mat 16:18 And I tell you, you are Peter, and on this rock <u>I will build my church,</u> and the gates of hell shall not prevail against it.

At the writing of the manuscript of this book, 9 Supreme Court justices approved 5 to 4 to make gay marriage the law of the land. We have come to a very critical time in the church in our nation. We must decide what we're going to stand for, what we're going to believe and how we're going to live. There are times when those decisions can be filled with shades of grey and we get by. There are times when those decisions can be delayed or even denied as we live in a time or season of compromise, not being fully committed to God or his principles, and not being totally sold out to the world. But then there are times when if we don't decide what we're going to stand for, what we're going to believe, and how we're going to live, it becomes the difference between our existence as a Church in the earth and our non-existence, our effectiveness as His body in the earth or our ineffectiveness. We're at that point in our world system and in the earth where the church must decide whether she's going to live by the world, or live by the Word.

The Church of Jesus Christ must decide whether or not she's going live in the natural or live in the supernatural realm through the blood of Jesus, by the power of the Holy Ghost. The Church of Jesus Christ must decide whether or not she's going to continue to live dependent on the world system or return to dependency on the system of the kingdom of God. The end is here, and the world we live in is testifying to that fact. Our world is reeling and rocking. Both in this nation and all over the world, both in our economic, political landscapes, and through disasters in the earth, seemingly caused by unusual weather patterns, the world we live in is testifying that the end is here.

Our world is on a downward spiral, fastly approaching the end of the age. The Gay marriage agenda in our nation is attempting to rewrite the moral code of the 10 commandments to redefine millenniums of human existence to fit this generation's unbridled lustful passions. The serpentine stranglehold of abortion continues to squeeze the life out of over 1.6 million wombs every year in our nation, wiping out nearly one-third of an entire generation born since 1973. The growing slave trade of pornography, homosexuality, human trafficking, and sexual perversion—not only accepted by the culture, but now shamelessly promoted by it—has claimed countless young men and women, pilfering the Kingdom of the Lord's inheritance. This is the context we find our world in as we approach the coming of the Lord. What's happening in our world? We are fast approaching the days of the generation of Lot. If God judged the generation of Lot, His word says He will necessarily need to judge this generation at the end of the age.

Come out from Among them

The only escape from the end-time Judgment on cities influenced by Jezebel during the generation at the end of the age, is to completely come out of the Jezebel, Harlot Babylonian system and obey the Lord, not based on seeing, but on faith, commanding your family to follow the Lord in the same manner, doing justice and judgment in your heart, not just in deed. (Genesis 18:19)

2 Corinthians 6:17 Wherefore come out from among them, and be ye separate, saith the Lord, and touch not the unclean thing; and I will receive you, 18 And will be a Father unto you, and ye shall be my sons and daughters, saith the Lord Almighty.

The Church – The Ecclesia of Christ

The Church must come out from among the system and the operation of Jezebel in the generation of the Lord's return. What we call the church and what Jesus calls the church are often two different definitions and expressions. What our westernized version of the church thinks of when we think of the church is a building, a Pastor, a service with singing, an offering, a sermon and an altar call. But what Jesus thinks of when he thinks of the church is something totally different. He thinks of a people that have come out of the world, out of the system of Jezebel, out of Harlot Babylon and have separated themselves unto Him, living by him, and one another (Acts 2:44-47). The Church is not a building, it's a person that has been brought out of the kingdom of Darkness by the renewing of their minds and has now been matured to receive the inheritance of keys to kingdom authority, the authority of the kingdom of heaven, to bring heaven to earth. The revelation of Christ in the Jewish mind and the revelation of Christ from the religious church mindset are often two different paradigms. The Jewish paradigm of the Church built upon a rock, is speaking of a judicial kingdom established on a throne to be the highest legislative court in the land, establishing justice in the earth for the oppressed through day and night prayer (Luke 18:1-8).

Mat 16:18 And I say also unto thee, That thou art Peter, <u>and upon this rock I will build my church;</u> and the gates of hell shall not prevail against it. <u>19 And I will give unto thee the keys of the kingdom of heaven: and whatsoever thou shalt bind on earth shall be bound in heaven: and whatsoever thou shalt loose on earth shall be loosed in heaven.</u>

When Jesus thinks of the Church He thinks of two primary things. He thinks of a legislative body for the establishing of justice in the earth. Number two, He thinks of a family, in which every believer when born into, is separated unto God and His kingdom.

The True Church of Jesus Christ vs. the Harlot Babylonian Church

The Church is a family of believers that have come out of the world system, and have separated themselves unto the Lord and the system of the kingdom of God for the establishing of justice in the earth. When Jesus said in Matthew 16:17 *"Upon this rock I will build MY Church,"* He wasn't talking about a building. He wasn't talking about a church service. He was talking about a people that would be taken out of the world system and be renewed in their minds to be separated unto the Lord for His kingdom purposes. The word church is the Greek word; *ekklēsia - ek-klay-see'-ah;* <u>*a calling out,*</u> *that is, (concretely) a popular meeting, especially a religious congregation (Jewish synagogue, or <u>Christian community</u> of members on earth or saints in heaven or both): - assembly, church.*

In Matthew chapter 16, the first Chapter where the word "Church" is mentioned in scripture, Jesus contrasts two separate mutually exclusive and diametrically opposed, *"called out ones,"* operating by two separate systems. In the first part of the chapter, beginning in verse 1, He shows His disciples *"the church"* – called out ones – that was operating in the Harlot Babylonian religious system of the Sadducees and Pharisees, and then later in verse 13 He reveals His called out ones (Church) that would operate by a revelation encounter with a Man, Christ Jesus, that would empower and prepare them to receive keys of authority to bind the kingdom and system of Babylon and loose and bring the kingdom of heaven to earth.

One system, the Harlot Babylonian system, would be subject to the spirit of Jezebel, and would be founded upon the spirit of adultery, characterized by the need for positon, prestige, fame, notoriety, and performance. One system would seek after signs and educational degrees to determine its validity, and the other system, the Kingdom of God, would be based on a revelation that would be characterized by true power and signs that follow, not the other way around. One system would be subject to the spirit of Jesus, which is the spirit of wisdom and revelation (Isaiah 11:1-3; Ephesians 1:17), and the other would be subject to the spirit of Jezebel, which is the spirit of manipulation, control and is a perversion of the true authentic church.

Mat 16:1 The Pharisees also with the Sadducees came, and tempting desired him that he would shew them a sign from heaven.

2 He answered and said unto them, When it is evening, ye say, It will be fair weather: for the sky is red.

3 And in the morning, It will be foul weather to day: for the sky is red and lowering. O ye hypocrites, ye can discern the face of the sky; but can ye not discern the signs of the times?

4 A wicked and adulterous generation seeks after a sign; and there shall no sign be given unto it, but the sign of the prophet Jonas. And he left them, and departed.

The Church represented by the Pharisees and Sadducees in Matthew 16:1-4, were an elite religious group that represented the spiritual leadership of God's people, the Jews, called out by God at Mount Sinai to be a light to the nations. But this elite religious group had corrupted themselves and had become a part of the generation Jesus called evil and adulterous. They had become interwoven with the spirit of Jezebel of that generation. They had become influenced by the system of Jezebel. They had become run by the spirit of Jezebel, which is the spirit that kills the prophets and replaces them with her own prophets, fed at her table.

1Ki 18:4 For it was so, <u>when Jezebel cut off the prophets of the LORD</u>, that Obadiah took an hundred prophets, and hid them by fifty in a cave, and fed them with bread and water.)

1Ki 18:13 Was it not told my lord what I did when <u>Jezebel slew the prophets of the LORD,</u> how I hid an hundred men of the LORD'S prophets by fifty in a cave, and fed them with bread and water?

1Ki 18:19 Now therefore send, and gather to me all Israel unto mount Carmel, and the <u>prophets of Baal four hundred and fifty, and the prophets of the groves four hundred, which eat at Jezebel's table</u>.

Rev 2:20 Notwithstanding I have a few things against thee, because <u>thou suffers that woman Jezebel, which calls herself a prophetess, to teach and to seduce my servants to commit fornication, and to eat things sacrificed unto idols.</u>

When Jesus began to reveal the system of the Kingdom of God in power and demonstration of the Holy Ghost, the Pharisees and Sadducees, those from the system of Harlot Babylon, came to Him to tempt him, asking him to show them a sign. This is one of the main characteristics of the Jezebel, Harlot Babylonian system. Those in this system requires some kind of sign before they will receive you. The Church that operates in the world system is built upon performance, your talent, abilities, or gifts. Its success standard is built upon how you look in the eyes of the people, how many you have following you, or how many members you have in your church. This is the foundation of the Jezebel spirit in the Church and is the source of the spirit of adultery and sexual perversion that is rampart in the church. It is the spirit of Jezebel, or as Jesus called them in verse 4, *an evil, wicked and adulterous generation.* Notice when they brought the woman caught in adultery to Jesus in John chapter 8, to see if He would judge her according to their law or standard, after Jesus exposes them, the religious elite, from the youngest to the oldest, were all also guilty of the same sin of adultery.

Joh 8:3 <u>And the scribes and Pharisees brought unto him a woman taken in adultery;</u> and when they had set her in the midst,

4 They say unto him, Master, <u>this woman was taken in adultery, in the very act.</u>

5 Now Moses in the law commanded us, that such should be stoned: but what sayest thou?

6 <u>This they said, tempting him, that they might have to accuse him.</u> But Jesus stooped down, and with his finger wrote on the ground, as though he heard them not.

7 So when they continued asking him, he lifted up himself, and said unto them, <u>He that is without sin among you, let him first cast a stone at her. 8 And again he stooped down, and wrote on the ground.</u>

9 <u>And they which heard it, being convicted by their own conscience, went out one by one, beginning at the eldest, even unto the last:</u> and Jesus was left alone, and the woman standing in the midst.

Notice, that every last one of them had fallen prey to sexual immorality, or the spirit of Jezebel. They were all a part of the spirit of the age from the youngest to the eldest. One of the main characteristics of this church system that leads to sexual sin or some kind of idol worship, of man, self, money, or materialism, is the temptation to operate in ministry by either your gift, your talent, or your educational degrees, or your pedigree, all to impress man, or to impress the people that you are leading. When you succumb to this temptation to perform for attention, success, notoriety, or fame in ministry, you have opened yourself up for the spirit of Jezebel to have access into your life to bring perversion and sin into your life and overtake the calling or assignment from God, for your own agenda or the agenda of Jezebel.

When the Pharisees and Sadducees came to Jesus in Matthew 16 to tempt Him, asking for a sign from Him before they would receive Him, Jesus said; *A wicked and adulterous generation seeks after a sign; and there shall no sign be given unto it, but the sign of the prophet Jonas. And he left them, and departed.*

Dying out to self and our selfish agendas defeats Jezebel

Jesus was saying to them, the only sign that you will receive to validate my ministry is my death, burial and resurrection. To overcome the spirit of Jezebel you must die out to self and the desires that are motivated by the Harlot Babylonian world system of notoriety, fame, power or prestige. Jesus was saying, I will not succumb to your temptation to perform for your approval or acceptance of me. Unless we're willing to die out to our flesh and how we look in the eyes of people we will not enter into the kingdom of God. Unless we're willing to become as nothing, or as a child in the eyes of those that are seeking to validate our assignments, we will not enter the kingdom of God, and we will never fulfill the assignment of God. Our willingness to submit to the death, burial and resurrection of our lives and assignments in God is the only sign of our calling in God, not our gifting or our abilities, nor our degrees.

Php 2:5 Let this mind be in you, which was also in Christ Jesus: 6 Who, being in the form of God, thought it not robbery to be equal with God: 7 But made himself of no reputation, and took upon him the form of a servant, and was made in the likeness of men: 8 And being found in fashion as a man, he humbled himself, and became obedient unto death, even the death of the cross. 9 Wherefore God also hath highly exalted him, and given him a name which is above every name:

God's ability to take our fallen nature and raise it up from the dust or the death of seeming failure in the eyes of people, should be the only sign of God's hand on our lives. And until we come out of any other expression and system that attempts to exalt man and His accomplishments over God and his kingdom, we will be subject to the spirit of Jezebel and be in danger of being judged by God and taken into great tribulation, right along with this Babylonian world system at the end of the age.

Rev 2:21 <u>And I gave her (Jezebel) space to repent of her fornication; and she repented not.</u> 22 <u>Behold, I will cast her into a bed, and them that commit adultery with her into great tribulation, except they repent of their deeds.</u> 23 And I will kill her children with death; and all the churches shall know that I am he which searches the reins and hearts: and I will give unto every one of you according to your works.

It's not enough to come out of the world in deed, refraining from certain behaviors that we publically associate with the spirit of the world, but we must come out of the spirit of the world and of Jezebel in our hearts, and in how we live and operate in life and in ministry when no one is looking. In order to come out we must not just come out, we must separate ourselves from that Jezebel system, and not touch the unclean thing, to be received as a son-daughter of the Lord Almighty.

The word "separate" is a Hebrew word "aphorize," which means to set boundaries. The word "touch" in 2Cor 6:17 is the Hebrew word "haptomai" which means; *to be set on fire*. When we set up boundaries then we can receive the fire of God that keeps the spirit of the world and of Jezebel from you. You can't come out and stay out of the spirit of the world without setting boundaries. But once you set boundaries then God can baptize you in a fire that keeps the Jezebel spirit at a noticeable distance from you.

How to Come out of the Jezebel Religious System

Beginning in verse 13 of Matthew 16 Jesus begins the process of leading his disciples into His Church and the purpose of the Church in the earth, out of the harlot Babylonian expression of the Church.

Mat 16:13 When Jesus came into the coasts of Caesarea Philippi, he asked his disciples, saying, <u>Whom do men say that I the Son of man am?</u>

14 And they said, some say that thou art John the Baptist: some, Elias; and others, Jeremias, or one of the prophets.

15 He saith unto them, <u>But whom say ye that I am?</u>

16 And Simon Peter answered and said, <u>Thou art the Christ, the Son of the living God.</u>

17 And Jesus answered and said unto him, <u>Blessed art thou, Simon Barjona: for flesh and blood hath not revealed it unto thee, but my Father which is in heaven.</u>

18 And I say also unto thee, <u>That thou art Peter, and upon this rock I will build my church;</u> and the gates of hell shall not prevail against it.

19 <u>And I will give unto thee the keys of the kingdom of heaven: and whatsoever thou shalt bind on earth shall be bound in heaven: and whatsoever thou shalt loose on earth shall be locsed in heaven.</u>

The calling of believers out of the Harlot Babylonian system of Jezebel begins with a revelation of who Jesus is. Until you get a personal revelation of Jesus, that flesh and blood has not revealed unto you, you have not yet come out of the system of Jezebel and you are yet still subject to idol worship that blocks you from ever getting free from Jezebel. To get free from Jezebel you must get free from what flesh and blood thinks, what flesh and blood says, anc what flesh and blood reveals, the system that flesh and blood has established. Notice in verse 13 and 14, Jesus first asks His disciples, "Who do men (flesh and blood) say I am?" His disciples stated what flesh and blood was saying about who Jesus was; That He was John the Baptist, Elijah, and Jeremiah. While these three prophetic personalities were all a part of the process of the revealing of Jesus, they all pointed to and prophesied about His coming, but they were not Jesus. They were not the correct revelation of who Jesus was.

Some say you are John the Baptist

John the Baptist came preaching; Repent, for the kingdom of Heaven is at hand. This was the first step in preparing the way of the Lord to come to His people, and the people to receive Jesus as the Christ.

Mat 3:1 In those days came <u>John the Baptist, preaching in the wilderness of Judaea, 2 And saying, Repent ye: for the kingdom of heaven is at hand.</u> 3 For this is he that was spoken of by the prophet Esaias, saying, The voice of one crying in the wilderness, <u>Prepare ye the way of the Lord, make his paths straight.</u>

Notice that the message of John was formulated, given and preached in the wilderness, by a man that had come out of the religious system of his day, of the priesthood of his father, Zechariah, and the courts of the Pharisees and Sadducees. He was not taught, educated, nor trained in the religious system of the day, but by the spirit of God Himself, in the wilderness. Therefore, John's ministry qualified to prepare the way for Jesus' first coming. It's only those that come out of the religious system of Jezebel that will be qualified and positioned to prepare the way for the Lord's second return. However, regardless of how great John's ministry was, it was just a ministry of preparation to receive the revelation of Jesus Christ. John was not the Christ, and he had to continually reiterate that as his ministry progressed, because people began to think that this was what his ministry constituted, that He was the Messiah.

Joh 1:19 And this is the record of John, when the Jews sent priests and Levites from Jerusalem to ask him, Who art thou? 20 And he confessed, and denied not; but confessed, I am not the Christ.

John's Message of Repentance – Called out to go in

John's ministry did not constitute Him being the Messiah, nor did his ministry constitute the people being ushered into Christ's Church, it was preparation for being ushered into Christ's Church. Just because we sit under the preaching, teaching ministry of a great man of God, this does not mean we are members of the body of Christ. These ministries that teach and preach Jesus, should be preparation for you to encounter Christ for yourself, and it's at that point that you become a part of the body of Christ, or His Church. The message of repentance, which was the message John preached, is the process of the renewing of the mind towards the mind of Christ. This is the first step to receiving a revelation of who Christ is. But it (repentance) is not Christ, nor does this message make John the Christ. Therefore we should not stop at hearing from men and women of God, as if we receive them, we are in Christ, NO! These ministries and teachings should be leading us to Christ, to a personal encounter with Jesus Christ, which flesh and blood cannot reveal.

Some say you are Elijah

The second person that the people thought Jesus was, was Elijah, "*some say you are Elijah.*" Elijah was the prophet that came in power to confront the prophets of Baal in I Kings 18:19-41, in order to turn the hearts of the Fathers back to the children and the hearts of the children back to the fathers (Mal. 4:5). This was the second step in the process of receiving a revelation of who Christ was, but it did not constitute Elijah being the Christ.

1Ki 18:19 Now therefore send, and gather to me all Israel unto mount Carmel, and the prophets of Baal four hundred and fifty, and the prophets of the groves four hundred, which eat at Jezebel's table.

1Ki 18:24 And call ye on the name of your gods, and I will call on the name of the LORD: and the God that answers by fire, let him be God.

Mal 4:5 Behold, I will send you Elijah the prophet before the coming of the great and dreadful day of the LORD: 6 And he shall turn the heart of the fathers to the children, and the heart of the children to their fathers, lest I come and smite the earth with a curse.

The Power of Elijah – The Turning of our Hearts back to the Father

The people knew that Elijah the prophet would come in power before the Messiah, so they spent so much of their time looking for Elijah the prophet that they actually missed the Messiah when He was right in their midst. So because Jesus was operating in power, they thought this designated him, not as the Christ, but as Elijah But Elijah's power was supposed to lead them to the Messiah, not replace the Messiah. Therefore when the Pharisees and Sadducees sought after a sign from Jesus, to operate in some gift and power to prove who He was, he refused them. Why, because signs are to point you to your destination.

Signs are not the destination. The Jezebel system that they were operating in had them focused on prestige, power, position, not what they were in the position for, which was to lead and prepare the people for the Messiah. The second step in the process of receiving a revelation of Jesus Christ is POWER! But power is not the Church, neither does power constitute you being a part of the Church, but it is preparation for being ushered into Christ's Church. It's supposed to point you to a revelation of Jesus, not replace your pursuit after Jesus. Many in the Jezebel, Harlot Babylon system of this generation spend more time pursuing power than they do Jesus.

….And Others Jeremiah

The last prophet the people thought Jesus was, was Jeremiah the weeping prophet. This prophet was the prophet that wept for the state and the coming judgment of Israel, and out of that great burden for Israel He prophesied that judgment upon his own nation. Because Jesus wept over Jerusalem, and because He prophesied the desolation of Jerusalem, they thought He was the Prophet Jeremiah. However, Jesus was not Jeremiah. Jeremiah's function of intercession and the fire of pronounced judgment over the state of Israel was the final process meant to prepare the believer to receive a revelation of Jesus as the Christ.

Mat 23:37 O Jerusalem, Jerusalem, thou that kills the prophets, and stones them which are sent unto thee, how often would I have gathered thy children together, even as a hen gathers her chickens under her wings, and ye would not! 38 Behold, your house is left unto you desolate. 39 For I say unto you, Ye shall not see me henceforth, till ye shall say, Blessed is he that cometh in the name of the Lord.

These 3 prophets are a process to the revelation of Jesus, but the people took these prophets as an end, rather than a means to an end, just as the 21st century Church also looks at her prophets. Even today in the Babylonian church system of the 21st century, many look at the process as the finished product of the church. We see the preaching ministries of John the Baptist as the Christ or the Church. This is not what constitutes His church. Or we see the power gifts of the Prophet Elijah as the Christ or purpose of the Church. And others think that the intercessory prayer ministry and the spirit's leading in prayer that brings forth the judgment of the world is the Christ, or purpose of the Church. But neither of these are the end of the Church, but the path to the door into a revelation of Christ, which brings the believer into the Church.

Notice in verse 16 and 17 in Matthew chapter 16, when Simon says, "You (Jesus) are the Christ the son of the Living God," Jesus Blesses Him, changes his name and then tells him, *"Flesh and Blood did not reveal this unto you."* You can't get this from a position close to the religious leaders. You can't get this from a man's teaching. To ascertain this revelation of Christ the Son of the Living God, it has to come from MY FATHER IN HEAVEN.

The Purpose of the Church: To call us out to give us Kingdom Authority

God's purpose in giving us a revelation of Jesus is to make us the Church. It's the means by which we are brought into the Church. It's not until we receive the revelation of Jesus Christ, which is revealed by our heavenly father, that we become the Church. The goal and purpose of the Church is bringing the believer out of the Jezebel expression of the Harlot Babylonian world system, by a revelation of Jesus and His kingdom, to be given authority to bind Jezebel and her prophets, and release the kingdom of God into the earth. The revelation of Jesus is what separates us and calls us out of the Kingdom of the darkness of this Babylonian world system. This is what causes us to begin to identify with our heavenly heritage and releases unto us our spiritual inheritance of the keys of authority to unlock and release the kingdom of God, and bind the kingdom of darkness. Our identity is changed from our earthly association and connection to our natural families, to our heavenly identity and association with our spiritual family. Our new identity comes from a revelation of Jesus as Messiah. This identity is connected to His mission as Messiah of building His kingdom on the earth. Therefore, the purpose of the Church (coming out of the Jezebel system) is to receive keys of authority to prepare the way for the coming of the Lord and His kingdom, through prayer in the earth – Binding the Kingdom of Darkness and Loosing the Kingdom of Heaven.

Mat 16:18 And I say also unto thee, That thou art Peter, <u>and upon this rock I will build my church</u>; and the gates of hell shall not prevail against it. 19 <u>And I will give unto thee the keys of the kingdom of heaven:</u> and whatsoever thou shalt bind on earth shall be bound in heaven: and whatsoever thou shalt loose on earth shall be loosed in heaven.

We can't do this until we come away from Jezebels table. We can't overcome Jezebel until we come out of her political and religious system. Therefore, He says come out from among them and be ye separate says the Lord, touch not the unclean thing and I will receive you unto myself, and I will be your father and you shall be my sons and daughters says the almighty God (2 Corinthians 6).

Holiness – The Call of Our Cities

God wants His Church to be Houses of Prayer to pray, to release God's kingdom and purposes for Cities. These prayers are going to be what spares whole cities from the Judgment of the Jezebel, Harlot Babylon system. After God revealed to me the meaning of the spirit of Leviathan, Jezebel and Python and how these spirits are holding whole cities in its grips and tentacles, God began dealing with me about Holy Cities, and how cities can overcome the manifestation of the principality of the spirit of Jezebel and the judgment of cities at the end of the age.

> *Rev 21:10 And he carried me away in the spirit to a great and high mountain, and shewed me that* **great city, the holy Jerusalem**, *descending out of heaven from God.*

In Revelation 21:2 John says, "I John, saw the holy city, New Jerusalem, coming down from God out of heaven as a bride adorned for husband…..having the glory of God: and her light was like unto a stone most precious, even like a jasper stone, clear as crystal." I believe that it is the purpose of the people of God to be builders of Cities, not churches. The building of the Church is the function of Christ, the Head. Jesus said, *"Upon this Rock **I will** build **My Church**."* The function of the church, his people in the earth, is to build cities, filling them with the glory of God, and the principles of the kingdom of God, making them Holy, and New. (Matt 16:19) *"Whatsoever ye bind/loose on* earth/heaven will be bound/loosed in Heaven/earth.) Jesus does not make anything or anyone holy, that's the job of those that come into contact and intimacy with a Holy God. He says; *be ye Holy, as I am Holy*. It's our command to be Holy, and it's our responsibility to make our cities Holy. This holiness is not just talking about morality and sin issues, but it speaks of the callings and purposes of people and cities. Holiness deals with distinctiveness and uniqueness of persons, their call and their purpose. God is holy because there's none like him. He's unique; He's distinct, other than, completely separate from any other.

What is Holiness?

Holiness deals with fulfilling your distinct purpose and walking in your distinct calling in the earth. Each individual has a unique purpose and calling that no one else has, and each city has a unique purpose and calling that no one else has or can fulfill. The New Jerusalem being a Holy City speaks directly to its purpose being restored and it's calling being fulfilled. What is the purpose and calling of Jerusalem? The word "*Jerusalem*" is a word that in the Hebrew means; *founded on peace, or the city of peace*. SO THE PURPOSE OF JERUSALEM IS TO BE A CITY OF PEACE. THE CALLING OF JERUSALEM IS TO BRING PEACE TO THE WORLD. Presently in 2015 everyone knows that Jerusalem in not a city of peace. It is the most tumultuous, divisive, dangerously violent city in the earth. It's full of strife, bitterness, hatred, division, wars and threats and rumors of war, as the two brothers from Abraham - *Isaac and Ishmael* - fight over the promise land. It is because the spirit of Leviathan, Jezebel and Python has intertwined with that city's destiny and calling, and has influenced rulers and leaders for centuries and millenniums with its flattery, deceit, and its corrupt commerce. However, the vision that John saw in the revelation was a vision of a New Jerusalem, a Holy City, and a city, whose walls were rebuilt. Rebuilt walls means that the fighting, strife, and division had ceased and the threat of war had been erased. In scripture walls around a city were deterrents for war, for intruders, invaders, for enemies. A city without walls was a place open to enemy invasion and a place where anything and everything goes.

> **Pro 25:28** *He that hath no rule over his own spirit is like a city that is broken down, and without walls.*

What walls were rebuilt in the city of Jerusalem making it a Holy, new City? They were the walls of Intercession. Isaiah 62:6 says *I have set watchmen on your walls, O Jerusalem; they shall never hold their peace day or night...till He makes Jerusalem a praise in the earth.* Intercession for the city of Jerusalem to become a Holy City, and a praise in the earth, is one of the vital attributes of the walls of the city being rebuilt, and at the return of Heaven to earth at the end of Human History, it is what enabled this city to be seen as a New City, a Holy City, a City founded on its purpose of peace and oneness of spirit, soul and body.

This is what is referred to when God speaks of a Holy City; its' referring to that city or persons in that city fulfilling the distinct purpose and calling for that city or nation, or for their life. For a city to be made new what's holding that city from its purpose must be removed. God told me it's the spirit of Jezebel that is holding my city from its purposes. Until we focus on rebuilding the walls of our cities, we will not see the Glory of God. I believe the new thing that God is doing in the earth is that he's transitioning His church from being builders of churches to being builders of Cities, filling them with the glory of God. If the new thing is the Church building cities and filling them with the Glory of God, as opposed to building buildings and filling them with people, until we get our minds off of coming to church **_to see_** the glory of God and get it on leaving the church **_to be_** the glory of God we will not see our Cities changed by the power of God. Until we get free from the spirit of Jezebel we will never truly see the glory of God in our lives or our cities.

CHAPTER 4

NOT ASHAMED OF THE GOSPEL OF CHRIST

Rom 1:16 For I am not ashamed of the gospel of Christ: for it is the power of God unto salvation to everyone that believes; to the Jew first, and also to the Greek.

It goes without saying that we are living in perilous times. With the recent Supreme Court ruling making gay marriage the law of the land, our nation has opened up the floodgates of the rising tide of immorality and perversion. These times reveal signs that we're living in the last days. Paul gives characteristics of the last days in 2 Tim. 1-7, and with the increase and escalation of these characteristics it is clear that we are coming near to the end of the age. Paul says;

2Ti 3:1 This know also, that in the last days perilous times shall come. 2 For men shall be lovers of their own selves, covetous, boasters, proud, blasphemers, disobedient to parents, unthankful, unholy,

3 Without natural affection, trucebreakers, false accusers, incontinent, fierce, despisers of those that are good, 4 Traitors, heady, high-minded, lovers of pleasures more than lovers of God;

5 Having a form of godliness, but denying the power thereof: from such turn away. 6 For of this sort are they which creep into houses, and lead captive silly women laden with sins, led away with divers lusts, 7 Ever learning, and never able to come to the knowledge of the truth.

What makes these times even more perilous is not the fact that men have become lovers of themselves, nor that they're without natural affection nor lovers of pleasures more than lovers of God. If that were all, the darkness of these vices would be no match for the light of the believers in God. But what makes these perilous times the last days is that these unnatural affections and lovers of pleasures actually have a form of godliness. What a form of godliness does is make the word of God of no effect.

Making the word of God of none effect through your tradition, which ye have delivered: Mar 7:13

A form of godliness accepts the existence of God but denies the power of God to effect a change and a transformation in the life of humanity. The times are perilous, not just because of the darkness that is pervading the landscape of our society and age, but because the purveyors of the light are actually participating in and contributing to the darkness with their form and traditions that keep the power of the light from shining bright. It's not what the unbelievers are doing that make these times perilous, but what the believers are doing. 2Ti 4:3 **For the time will come when they will not endure sound doctrine; but after their own lusts shall they heap to themselves teachers, having itching ears**; *4 And they shall turn away their ears from the truth, and shall be turned unto fables.*

The perilousness of these times are not the passing of the Supreme court decision to make gay marriage the law of the land, making sexual perversion the order of the day, nor is it the racial conflict happening throughout the nation and world, as nation prepares to come against nation in race wars like no other time in our nation's history. No! The perilousness of this time is that at a time when our nation needs the preaching of the gospel of Jesus Christ, the church of Jesus Christ has lost the true preaching of the gospel of Jesus Christ, and the power it possesses. This is because the church doesn't really know what the message of the gospel of Jesus Christ really is. We have lost the message of the gospel of Jesus Christ. The church of Jesus Christ is increasingly moving away from the preaching of the gospel of Jesus Christ.

Much of this moving away can be attributed to the spirit of Jezebel in society that is attempting to silence the voice of the Lords' prophets, both through the seducing into sexual sins of the servants of God participating in the same vice that Christ came to set us free from, and through the silencing of the prophets voices through increasing laws that legislates sin in society, prohibiting opposition and resistance to lifestyles that oppose God's laws, especially in regards to the perverse sexuality of sex outside of traditional marriage, and of homosexuality and lesbianism. If Jezebel can't inhibit, limit, pervert or completely stop the preaching of the gospel of Jesus Christ through legislating immoral laws, she most definitely will try to stop it through a lack of understanding and a perversion of what the message of Jesus Christ really is. In this, the spirit of perversion can completely take hold and totally collapse the foundations of humanity. Once this happens mankind is on the precipice of complete extinction. Which is what the forces of evil in the earth are after.

What is the True Preaching of the Gospel of Christ - Unashamed of Christ's Message

The only answer to the rising tide of immorality and perversion in our society is the true preaching of the gospel of Jesus Christ. The reason immorality and perversion is rising is because this generation has never truly heard the preaching of the true gospel of Jesus Christ. The word "Gospel" is a Greek word "Euaggelizō," which means; *to announce* **good news** *("evangelize") especially the gospel: - declare, bring (declare, show) glad (good) tidings, preach (the gospel) that means, "Good News."*

But all too often, instead of the church preaching good news, we've preached condemnation. We haven't preached condemnation intentionally. We've attempted to preach sanctification, or we've attempted to preach holiness, or we've attempted to preach righteousness. However, these doctrines are not messages that can be preached, or taught to impart, but these doctrines are revelations that are caught through the preaching of the gospel of Jesus Christ, of the Love that God has for the sinner, so much so, that He gave His only begotten Son. Once the sinner receives and believes this good news, and through the revelation of Christ receives His righteousness, this revelation will take the believer from faith to faith (Romans 1:17) to sanctification, victory over all sinful works of the flesh, and holiness. Holiness is something we do – Be ye Holy, as I am holy (I Peter 1:16) - only after we obtain a revelation of God's righteousness through Jesus Christ. When the gospel of Jesus Christ is not correctly understood and sufficiently preached, the context of society's morality grows unchecked until society becomes a cesspool of perversion, no matter how much we preach our holiness messages. The more society's immorality grows unchecked, with the good news of the gospel of Jesus Christ's love, the more uncomfortable it becomes for the Church to represent the ways and standards of God in society. Before long the ways and standard of Jesus Christ is completely resisted, until Jesus Christ is no longer looked at as one who came to bring good news, but as one who came to bring condemnation, hatred and unattainable laws.

Paul's Commitment to the Gospel in the midst of a Culture of Immorality

The context of Paul's famous statement and confession from Romans 1:16 – *I am not ashamed of the gospel of Jesus Christ* - was given in the context of a perverted, darkened society being overrun by the spirit of Jezebel through the perversion of Homosexuality and Lesbianism. In the midst of this counter-culture Paul proclaims his allegiance to the message of the good news of Christ's power to redeem the culture, saying;

Rom 1:16 For I am not ashamed of the gospel of Christ: for it is the power of God unto salvation to everyone that believes; to the Jew first, and also to the Greek. 17 For therein is the righteousness of God revealed from faith to faith: as it is written, the just shall live by faith.

Believers in Christ and scholars alike, familiar with these verses, fail to recognize that these verses are couched and contextualized within Paul's popular Romans 1 exposition about homosexuality and lesbianism. Paul is proclaiming his allegiance to the gospel of Christ in the context of the Romans having their minds darkened and perverted by the spirit of Jezebel, in favor of Homosexual and lesbian practices. Furthermore, most theological exegesis fails to recognize why Paul's so adamant about stating his unabashed, unapologetic, commitment to sharing this message to all, regardless of their lifestyle, their morality, or their comfort level with hearing it.

The Consequences of Not preaching the Gospel of Christ

Because Paul's statement of faith in the gospel of Christ is often taken out of its context when we read these verses we are unenlightened concerning Paul's emphasis on the consequences of their reluctance to preach the gospel of Jesus Christ to a heathen society. Firstly, the message of the gospel of Jesus Christ is good news to those bound in sins grips. Secondly, the gospel of Jesus Christ is the power of God unto Salvation. And thirdly, without the preaching of the good news of sins powerlessness to hold the hearer in its grips, the wrath of God will be released against all ungodliness and unrighteousness of them that hold the truth in unrighteousness. Let's read Romans 1:15-26 in its context in order to ascertain why he's indebted to and unashamed of preaching the gospel of Jesus Christ to the Gentiles of Rome.

*Rom 1:13 Now I would not have you ignorant, brethren, that oftentimes I purposed to come unto you, (but was let hitherto,) that I might have some fruit among you also, even as among **other Gentiles**.*

Rom 1:14 I am debtor both to the Greeks, and to the Barbarians; both to the wise, and to the unwise.

*Rom 1:15 So, as much as in me is, I am ready to preach the gospel **to you that are at Rome also**.*

*Rom 1:16 **For I am not ashamed of the gospel of Christ:** for it is the power of God unto salvation to everyone that believeth; to the Jew first, and also to the Greek.*

*Rom 1:17 For therein is the righteousness of God revealed from faith to faith: as it is written, **The just shall live by faith**.*

*Rom 1:18 **For the wrath of God is revealed from heaven against all ungodliness and unrighteousness of men, who hold the truth in unrighteousness;***

When Paul states in verse 15, "*I am ready to preach the gospel to you that are at Rome ALSO,*" he's actually distinguishing and highlighting the enormity of his task, and it's distinctiveness in comparison to the other cultures and Gentile nations he's heretofore preached the gospel to. Rome's culture was unlike any other culture Paul had evangelized. They were both sophisticated and fools all at the same time. They were both educated and ignorant, all at the same time. They were both darkened and enlightened all at the same time. Rome was a lot like the culture of our westernized generation in the 21st century. It was going to be his hardest, most difficult task to date. Paul knew that if the Church of Rome withheld the truth of Christ's redemptive work on the cross to release righteousness into the culture, in the midst of a culture of unrighteousness, the wrath of God would be revealed against all ungodliness and unrighteousness in that culture. But Paul was revealing his trump card – *The good news of the Gospel of the Grace of Jesus Christ to reveal the righteousness of God.*

The Gospel of Grace Reveals God's Righteousness to Unrighteous Humanity

These verses are detailing the importance and significance of the preaching of the gospel of the grace of Jesus Christ unto the Gentiles of Rome that are in moral darkness and behavioral decay, for the purpose of revealing the righteousness of God to them, which he says, is the power of God unto salvation. What is the righteousness of God, which verse 17 says, is revealed through the preaching of the gospel of Christ? And why is this significant to the message being preached to those that are struggling with their sexuality, their human sin nature and in moral behavioral decay?

The word righteousness comes from the original Greek word, "*dikaiosunē*" which means; *equity (of character or act); specifically (Christian) justification.* Justification means to be placed in right standing through the moral, equity and character of Christ. The good news is not only that Jesus died for our sins, but that His death, burial and resurrection brought us into right standing (righteousness) with God and gave us access to God to receive new life or a fresh start, before our behavior lines up with this reality. Therefore If I really believe, as a preacher of the good news of Jesus Christ, that Jesus died to bring the sinner into a righteous identity through the righteousness of God in Christ, then my job is not to preach you out of sin, my Job is to preach you out of the fear and condemnation that comes because of sin, about the consequences of sin, which is death. If Jesus died to save you from that penalty of sin, then there is now therefore no condemnation to those that receive and are in Christ Jesus (Rom. 8:1). Once you overcome the fear and condemnation associated with sins consequences, through a revelation of His righteousness, you no longer avoid him in your sin, but you run to him, even before your sinful behavior changes. When you feel you can come to him, even before your sinful behavior changes, you will eventually encounter the glorified Christ. Once you encounter Jesus, you won't want anything that you don't see on Jesus, and you'll want everything that you do see on Jesus.

The Righteousness of God – A Message of Identity, Love and Grace

The righteousness of God is the identity of the believer in Christ before God, in the eyes of God, because of Jesus Christ. The righteousness of God is how God sees every person, both unbelievers and believers alike, in Jesus Christ. When the unbeliever is told that God is not mad at them, and that he loves them, this is part of the good of the gospel of Jesus Christ. This is in essence a message of Hope and Love. God no longer sees or relates to humanity after their behavior or after their sin nature, but through a new righteousness nature revealed and made possible through the death, burial and resurrection of Jesus Christ. This is the good news of the gospel – *the righteousness of God* - that is supernaturally revealed to the hearer at the preaching of the good news of this message, called the gospel of Grace, or the good news of Jesus Christ. This message is good news because it reveals the Love God has for humanity, the extent to which He went to express this Love, and that God is no longer relating with us based on our sin nature or our behavior. God relates to us based on and through Jesus Christ and what he did at the cross. This message that reveals from God this revelation of righteousness, releases a new identity to the hearer as a son or daughter of God, in spite of our behavior not yet being changed. This new identity, is what is referred to in scripture, as being *"Born Again"* (John 3:3) into son-ship. And this born-again experience can only come through the preaching of the gospel of Jesus Christ.

Joh 1:12 But as many as received him, to them gave he power to become the sons of God, even to them that believe on his name: 13 Which were born, not of blood, nor of the will of the flesh, nor of the will of man, but of God.

Righteousness or Wrath – God's Wrath is released where God's Righteousness is not Preached

It's this preaching that causes God's nature and identity as sons of God to be revealed to our perverted, distorted human nature, which all of us have inherited through birth, as a result of our first parents' Adam and Eve's sin. Without the preaching of the gospel of Jesus Christ, revealing the righteousness of God as our new identity in Christ by faith, there can be no understanding of God's love, there can be no good news associated with God's word, and there can be no deliverance from the condemnation associated with our old sin nature. It is by the preaching of the gospel of Jesus Christ, of the Father God's nature to *SO LOVE THE WORLD,* which releases a new revelation from Christ of the Father and a new revelation of Christ from the Father. This is what happened to Peter and the disciples when Christ was revealed to them in Matthew 16:13-17

Mat 16:17 And Jesus answered and said unto him, Blessed art thou, Simon Barjona: **for flesh and blood hath not revealed it unto thee**, but my Father which is in heaven.

Until Christ is revealed to humanity there can be no conversion, deliverance or change of nature. But until the true Christ of the Cross with His substitutionary sacrifice is preached Christ can't be revealed. It's this message that is good news, that when preached reveals the righteousness of God from the faith of the presenter with the revelation, to the faith of the hearer or receiver by revelation. This is what Paul refers to in Romans 1:17 when he says, *the righteousness of God is revealed from faith to faith.* It's the faith of the one preaching the good news, releasing the message that causes the revelation of righteousness to be received by faith of the one hearing the good news, that God so loved the world, that he gave His only begotten Son, that whosoever believes in Him, shall not perish but have everlasting life.

What is the Gospel of Jesus Christ – *The Spirit of Life in Christ Jesus has made us free from the law of sin and death- Ro 8:2*

This is why Paul was stressing that he and we must not be ashamed of the gospel of Jesus Christ. What is there to be ashamed of? But we must answer the question, what is the Gospel of Jesus Christ? This must be the very center issue in the preaching of the gospel in our modern expression of Christianity. If we are going to overcome the spirit of Jezebel and bring light to a dark world we must get the message right. There is a dearth in America for the preaching of the word of God in our Christian expression of the Church of Jesus Christ in 21st century Christianity. We are emphasizing and becoming fat off of junk food in the body of Christ, focusing on and emphasizing side doctrines or fringe messages that focus on the believer in Christ getting bigger, better and the best in this materialistic, ME driven society. In our Christian world today humanity's pleasures and our focus on these pleasures, have taken center stage in the Church of Jesus Christ, while the centrality of the message of Jesus Christ has become an afterthought or a side bar. Faith for things and prosperity for my house, car and bank account is the order of the day, while faith for Jesus to return and His kingdom to come and will to be done in earth, as recorded in Luke 18:8 and Matt 6:10, have almost been considered trivial and non-essential in this modern, so-called enlightened, progressive Christianity.

Nevertheless when the Son of man cometh, shall he find faith on the earth? Luk 18:8

Mat 6:10 Thy kingdom come. Thy will be done in earth, as it is in heaven.

Returning to the Preaching of the Message of the Love of God

What is the good news of the gospel of Jesus Christ that must be preached to release the revelation of the righteousness of God to humanity? Jesus gave us this message straight from His own mouth in John 3:16-18

Joh 3:16 For God so loved the world, that he gave his only begotten Son, that whosoever believeth in him should not perish, but have everlasting life.

Joh 3:17 For God sent not his Son into the world to condemn the world; but that the world through him might be saved.

Joh 3:18 He that believeth on him is not condemned: but he that believeth not is condemned already, because he hath not believed in the name of the only begotten Son of God.

The good news of the gospel of Jesus Christ is that God so loved the World, that he gave His only begotten Son, and that whoever believes in him shall not perish but have everlasting life. This message is about the great love of God. But the key to the message actually releasing the good news of God's love to its hearers is that it must be preached by those that have the Love of God. In order to impart the love of God you must have the Love of God to impart it to the hearers. In order to preach the true gospel of Jesus Christ, you have to have the Love of God. Not only must you have Love for God, but you must have God's love for the world. It's the first and second great commandments that we are promised we will have.

Mat 22:37 And he said to him, "__You shall love the Lord your God__ with all your heart and with all your soul and with all your mind. 38 This is the great and first commandment. 39 And a second is like it: __You shall love your neighbor as yourself.__

I can't preach the message of God's love to a sinner unless and until I love them like God loves them. Before I can reach a sinner I must love the sinner. Unless I love the sinner that I attempt to preach to, the sinner will hear the message of Love wrapped in a package of condemnation. But when I love the person I'm preaching the love of God to, this message not only becomes good news to the hearer, but it releases that love to the hearer. Therefore, the message of the love of God can only be good news when it comes from someone that loves the hearer with the love of God.

This message can only be considered good news if it is couched in the context of the law of sin and death. *Romans 8:2 For the law of the Spirit of life in Christ Jesus hath made me free from the law of sin and death.*

The essence of what the law of sin and death says, in the New Testament, can be found in Romans 6:23. It says, *"For the wages of sin is death……"* This verse doesn't stop there, but were going to interrupt that verse right there for now, to parenthetically instate that sin is not something we do, it's something we were ALL born with. *Psa. 51:5 Behold, I was shapen in iniquity; and in sin did my mother conceive me.* Sin is a virus that we were infected with because the blood we were born with was contaminated because of our first parents, Adam and Eve. Therefore, we were all born with a death sentence over our lives because the payday of Adam's sin, pronounced before he ever committed the sin, is death (Gen 2:16). *And the LORD God commanded the man, saying, of every tree of the garden thou may freely eat: 17 But of the tree of the knowledge of good and evil, thou shalt not eat of it:* **for in the day that you eat thereof thou shalt surely die.**

We were all born into sin. But the good news of the gospel is that Jesus Christ was not born with Adam's blood, nor his death sentence, because He was born of a virgin who had never known a man. It's the man that determines the blood type as well as the sex of a baby. But Jesus was not born of a man, only a woman, impregnated by the Holy Ghost.

Luk 1:26 And in the sixth month the angel Gabriel was sent from God unto a city of Galilee, named Nazareth,

Luk 1:27 To a virgin espoused to a man whose name was Joseph, of the house of David; and the virgin's name was Mary.

Luk 1:28 And the angel came in unto her, and said, Hail, thou that art highly favoured, the Lord is with thee: blessed ort thou among women.

Luk 1:29 And when she saw him, she was troubled at his saying, and cast in her mind what manner of salutation this should be.

Luk 1:30 And the angel said unto her, Fear not, Mary: for thou hast found favour with God.

Luk 1:31 And, behold, thou shalt conceive in thy womb, and bring forth a son, and shalt call his name JESUS.

Luk 1:32 He shall be great, and shall be called the Son of the Highest: and the Lord God shall give unto him the throne of his father David:

Luk 1:33 And he shall reign over the house of Jacob for ever; and of his kingdom there shall be no end.

Luk 1:34 Then said Mary unto the angel, How shall this be, seeing I know not a man?

Luk 1:35 And the angel answered and said unto her, The Holy Ghost shall come upon thee, and the power of the Highest shall overshadow thee: therefore also that holy thing which shall be born of thee shall be called the Son of God.

Because Jesus was not born of a man, His blood was sinless, therefore His blood could be offered up for a blood transfusion for the sins of humanity, to give mankind life for sin in the place of death for sin (Romans 6:23)

The good news is that because Jesus Christ, the Son of God, came and died in our place for our sins, we don't have to die the way we were born. Because even though the wages of sin is death….*the gift of God is eternal life through Jesus Christ our Lord. Romans 6:23*

Rom 8:1 There is therefore now no condemnation to them which are in Christ Jesus, who walk not after the flesh, but after the Spirit.

Rom 8:2 For the law of the Spirit of life in Christ Jesus hath made me free from the law of sin and death.

Rom 8:3 For what the law could not do, in that it was weak through the flesh, God sending his own Son in the likeness of sinful flesh, and for sin, condemned sin in the flesh:

Rom 8:4 That the righteousness of the law might be fulfilled in us, who walk not after the flesh, but after the Spirit.

In these verses the Apostle Paul is writing to the church in Rome, relaying the message that if humanity hears the good news of the gospel that Jesus Christ came and died for our sins, so that we would not have to pay the penalty of that sin, and believe that message, there is no longer anymore condemnation for our sins, for those that choose to believe, associate, and give themselves to Jesus Christ and His work of atonement for our sins.

Understanding this Message as Good News

For this to be understood as good news, think of it like this. If you were tried and convicted of a crime that you knew you committed and the sentence of the crime was life in prison, but before they could come back with the verdict, the lawyers came and told you some unsuspecting person all of a sudden showed up out of the blue and confessed to the crime that you know you committed, and their prints or DNA matched the ones at the crime scene, therefore you're free to go, how would that make you feel? Would you be grateful, thankful, or relieved? How would you thank that person? What would you want to say to that person? Would you want to know why they took the blame for a crime you know you committed? Would you visit them in prison if they wanted you to? The average person would not only want to know and do all of that, but even more. The average person would be willing to establish a bond with that person, receiving the letters from that person. The average person would write back and look to live and do the best they could to make the sacrifice that person made for them count.

This is good news to the sinner. But if there is no sin, or sin has not been confessed and called sin, If we label our sins as our preferences, or our inclinations or proclivities, which are a part of our human nature to which we should not, could not or must not be held accountable for as being wrong, we negate the work of the forgiveness, cleansing and healing of sin through the blood of Jesus, and there's no more forgiveness of sins, but wrath for sins.

When the Good News of the Gospel is not preached

The wrath of God increases when those that have the truth, hold onto the truth because they are ashamed of the gospel of truth in the midst of a culture that despises and resists anything that challenges their behavior. When those that hold the truth in unrighteousness give in to the unrighteous lifestyles of those that are unwilling to hear and believe the truth, it releases the wrath of God, which is the increase of God's judgment on ungodliness and unrighteousness in a region. Paul is saying, it's my preaching of Jesus Christ that holds back the wrath of God against ungodliness and unrighteousness. *I MUST PREACH JESUS TO HOLD BACK GOD'S WRATH AGAINST A SINFUL AND UNGODLY GENERATION.*

The Just shall live by Faith

Again, this message of Jesus Christ, revealing the righteousness of God, is what shows the heathen their new identity, irrespective of their behavioral change. Their behavior won't change until the message of Jesus changes their identity, and how they see themselves before God. God loves them, because of Jesus. God loves them through Jesus, and God wants to show and release to them His love, and it begins with the preaching of the good news of the gospel of Jesus. God wants them to know that he's not mad at them because of their behavior. God wants them to know that he's not judging them because of their behavior, because Jesus has already taken that Judgment on himself on the cross. Once this message is preached and God's righteousness – right standing – is revealed, God begins to change the identity of those who have this righteousness revealed to them. Once this identity change happens, where the hearer of the message realizes that they are now rightly connected to God as His sons and daughters, soon after, their behavior will begin to change to line up to God's original intent for humanity created in the image of God. When we know that we are loved by God, irrespective of our behavior or performance, it empowers us to live for God. God changes our Human, sinful nature through His unconditional love for us. Until this change happens, Paul says, in verse 17; *THE JUST SHALL LIVE BY FAITH.*

This is saying that those that have come to the revelation of the righteousness of God through faith in Jesus, until their behavior changes, they will live by Jesus' behavior and what He did for them, and by His righteousness, and not their own righteousness or good works. They will live by what Jesus did for them on Calvary, not by what they do from day to day. They will live by the faith that one day their lives are going to change to line up with the Christ nature that has been imparted to them at the preaching of Jesus Christ. Romans 10:17 says, this faith comes by continuing to hear the message of Jesus Christ. The more you hear, learn and believe about all that Christ did and gave to us through His word, the more your behavior will begin to change to line up to what you're hearing, learning and believing. This process of faith in the preaching of the gospel of righteousness, or the gospel of grace, will steadily change the culture and climate of a sinful nation, or generation.

What is the Wrath of God released on those that hold the truth in ungodliness?

If the gospel is not preached and-or the gospel of God's righteousness is not received by the hearers in any nation or generation where the truth of the gospel is available to be preached, Paul calls this, holding the truth in unrighteousness. And he says, God's wrath is revealed against all ungodliness and unrighteousness on those who do such. This is the agenda of the work of the spirit of Jezebel, to silence the preaching of the gospel, so the God of Jehovah has no access into society and is therefore not worshipped, but only her sexual, perverted Idol gods of Baal. In Romans 1 verses 19 - 32 Paul shows them what this wrath and judgment will look like, to both the believer and unbeliever alike;

Rom 1:19 Because that which may be known of God is manifest in them; for God hath shewed it unto them.

Rom 1:20 For the invisible things of him from the creation of the world are clearly seen, being understood by the things that are made, even his eternal power and Godhead; so that they are without excuse:

Rom 1:21 Because that, when they knew God, they glorified him not as God, neither were thankful; but became vain in their imaginations, and their foolish heart was darkened.

Rom 1:22 Professing themselves to be wise, they became fools,

Rom 1:23 And changed the glory of the incorruptible God into an image made like to corruptible man, and to birds, and four-footed beasts, and creeping things.

Rom 1:24 Wherefore God also gave them up to uncleanness through the lusts of their own hearts, to dishonor their own bodies between themselves:

Rom 1:25 Who changed the truth of God into a lie, and worshipped and served the creature more than the Creator, who is blessed forever. Amen.

Rom 1:26 For this cause God gave them up unto vile affections: for even their women did change the natural use into that which is against nature:

Rom 1:27 And likewise also the men, leaving the natural use of the woman, burned in their lust one toward another; men with men working that which is unseemly, and receiving in themselves that recompense of their error which was meet.

Rom 1:28 And even as they did not like to retain God in their knowledge, God gave them over to a reprobate mind, to do those things which are not convenient;

Rom 1:29 Being filled with all unrighteousness, fornication, wickedness, covetousness, maliciousness; full of envy, murder, debate, deceit, malignity; whisperers,

Rom 1:30 Backbiters, haters of God, despiteful, proud, boasters, inventors of evil things, disobedient to parents,

Overcoming the spirit of Jezebel

Rom 1:31 Without understanding, covenant-breakers, without natural affection, implacable, unmerciful:

Rom 1:32 Who knowing the judgment of God, that they which commit such things are worthy of death, not only do the same, but have pleasure in them that do them.

CHAPTER 5

PERSONAL TRANSFORMATION THE REVELATION OF GOD'S RIGHTEOUSNESS AND THE GOSPEL OF GRACE

Rom 6:11 So you also must consider yourselves dead to sin and alive to God in Christ Jesus. 12 Let not sin therefore reign in your mortal body, to make you obey its passions. 13 Do not present your members to sin as instruments for unrighteousness, but present yourselves to God as those who have been brought from death to life, and your members to God as instruments for righteousness. 14 For sin will have no dominion over you, since you are not under law but under grace.

Romans 6 is the most important chapter in the New Testament on personal transformation. It is completely focused on that. In this chapter Paul tells us, as believers, how we can access the power of God, how we can experience it in our everyday life. I am going to focus particularly on overcoming sexual perversion in our battle against sexual sin.

Romans 6:1-10: Our legal position speaks of how God sees us and relates to us in Christ and the benefits that we freely and fully received at our new birth because of what Jesus did on the cross. Paul describes our legal position in Christ. In other words, what we have received by being in Christ—the benefits that are ours. Romans 6:11-14: We cooperate with grace by fully embracing three primary principles—they are to know truth (v. 11), resist darkness (v. 12-13a), and pursue loving God and people (v. 13b).

Paul urged us not to receive grace in vain by neglecting to lay hold of it (2 Cor. 6:1). The part we are going to focus in on in this chapter is how to cooperate with the grace of God that is described as available to us in verse 1-10. It is not enough that the grace of God is available; we want to experience it. We want to experience it in our everyday life, and we want to be empowered by it to overcome sexual perversion. Paul outlines three particular principles.

These are the primary principles that are necessary for us to access the power of God, so that our mind and emotions can walk free from the dominion of sinful emotions and sinful thinking that produce sexual sins and perversion. We cannot choose one of these three principles above the others. We need to embrace all three of them and do them consistently. Now having said that, even in consistency, our doing of these principles is flawed and weak. We do them in our humanity. The Lord understands that, and that is enough. In our weak and broken way we embrace these three principles.

Then what happens as a result over time embracing these three principles are described in the final part of Romans 6:15-23. It describes our living condition. Romans 6:15-23: Our living condition speaks of how we live in our daily life—how much grace we experience in our mind and emotions as they are renewed by interacting with the Holy Spirit. When we are changed on the inside, then our behavior on the outside follows suit. So verse 15-23 describes what happens in our mind and our emotions.

Paul assures that anyone who engages in the three principles set forth in verses 11-13 will experience victory over sin—sin shall not have dominion over their mind and emotions (v. 14a). We will have victory in a substantial way in this age and in an absolute way in the age to come.

11...reckon [see] yourselves to...be alive to God in Christ...12. Therefore do not let sin reign in your mortal body...13. And do not present your members...to sin, but present yourselves to God...14. For sin shall not have dominion over you, for you are not under law but under grace. (Rom. 6:11-14)

Paul assures us that any believer who engages consistently in these three principles will experience victory over the dominion of sin in their mind and their emotions and, therefore, in their character and outward behavior. Paul promises in verse 14 that sin shall not have dominion over us. In this context particularly, he is talking about sin not having dominion over our mind and our emotions.

As believers, our mind and emotions still have the taint of sin in them. Paul said that you have the resources in the grace of God to actually walk in a way where this taint of sin in your mind, emotions, and body will not have dominion over you (Rom. 6:11-14, paraphrased). It will not control you. Yes, we will fight against it. We will resist it, but we will have the upper hand instead of the negative emotions and feelings having the upper hand in our lives. Paul promises us this victory— that sin shall not have dominion over us.

Now the victory that he promises is a substantial victory in this age. It is not perfect, but it is substantial, with an absolute complete victory in the age to come. The problem is that many believers have experienced so much defeat. They love the Lord. Many of them have been walking with the Lord for decades, and they are giving up on the idea that they are really going to have freedom from the dominion of negative feelings and thought patterns. So Paul is wanting to convince them through Romans 6 that righteousness is not only attractive in the liberty and the fruitfulness of righteousness, but it is doable.

It is within the reach of every single believer, no matter how broken you have been in your past. He is saying that the power of God and the grace of God are actually stronger than the negative sinful patterns we have had in days past. Principle number one: In verse 11, Paul says, *"Reckon yourself to be dead to sin, but alive to God."* To reckon ourselves is to see ourselves in the way that God sees us in Christ. We have to know certain things, and it takes time to cultivate that knowledge.

Paul said that we are transformed by renewing our mind—by knowing the things we must know. It is not enough to know things. We have to resist things—negative things, sinful urges, temptations, and situations. It says in Rom. 6:12, *"Do not let sin reign in your body."* He goes on and adds to it, *"Do not present yourself to sin; do not let it reign and do not put yourself in a position that sin is stirred up in your life"* (Rom. 6:12-13, paraphrased).

So we have to know some things, and we have to resist some things. He goes on in the end of verse 13 to say, *"Present yourself to God."* We have to present ourselves; we have to pursue things. We have to pursue

God. We have to pursue the activities that obey the will of God and kingdom activities as well. Paul gives the promise in verse 14 (paraphrased). "If you will do these three," he says, "I want to promise you sin will not have dominion over your mind and emotions. Yes, the taint of sin will be there, but it will not rule you. It will not be the primary dominant force in your life."

He says, "You will have ability to overcome it. You will have ability to live in substantial freedom on the inside and on the outside if you will do these three principles consistently, sincerely" (Rom. 6:14, paraphrased). Again, lest you say that you are never going to be able to do that—when we do them, we do them flawed. We do these principles in weakness; that is the only option we have. So that is still workable. It still works if people like you and me engage in these principles in a sincere and a consistent way, though in a flawed and imperfect way. He continues in verse 14, and here is a very key phrase or truth.

He said that the reason sin will not dominate your mind and emotions is because of this truth: you are not under law, but you are under grace. Now this phrase, you are not under law but you are under grace, is a very, very powerful phrase that has many implications. I will say as well that this is a phrase that is often misquoted, misunderstood, and misapplied. In the context here Paul is talking about how you have the power to resist sin. He is imparting vision to walk in righteousness. He is saying that righteousness is attractive and doable because you are under grace. Some people understand the grace of God as the exact opposite. They believe that, because they are under grace, it does not matter if they walk in righteousness. Paul has the exact different approach. In other words, he is saying, "Because you are under grace, righteousness is doable in your everyday lifestyle. It is your destiny. It is your inheritance to walk free from the dominion of this negative influence on the inside."

The Three Principles for Experiencing Victory over Sin

The three principles are—
1. To know who we are in Christ (v. 11),
2. To resist darkness (v. 12-13a), and
3. To pursue loving God and people (v. 13b).

There is no substitute for any of these principles. These three principles are the context for experiencing victory.

Paul used the word "for" twice in verse 14. In the first "for" Paul promised victory to all (v. 12). In the second "for" he gives the basis for this victory—because we are not under law, but under grace. In other words, because of our new acceptance, position, power, and destiny in Christ (v. 1-11).

We Are Not Under Law

We are no longer under the condemnation or powerlessness of the law. Being under the law means to attempt to earn salvation by our deeds and to seek to live godly by the power of our flesh. Being under law means to relate to God based on how well we are doing. We are not under law. There are many implications of what it means that we are not under the law. I am only going to mention a couple of them here. Not being under the law means we are not under the condemnation of the law. We are not under condemnation before God. This means that God enjoys us, God delights in us, and God enjoys our relationship with Him. The enemy comes and tells us just the opposite—that God is at the very end of His patience; just one more mess up and that is it!

Paul says, "No, you are not at all under the condemnation that you were under when you were under the law before you were in Christ" (Rom. 6:14; Romans 8:1-2, paraphrased). Everybody, before they are born again, is under the law in their relationship before God. It is not only that they are free from condemnation, but they are also no longer powerless—meaning by virtue of the Holy Spirit living in their born-again spirit, they actually have a resource to challenge negative emotions if they interact with that resource. And that resource is a person called the Holy Spirit. Being under law also means it is the attempt to earn one's salvation by good deeds. Everybody outside of Christ—they are trying and hoping they will be saved or everything will go well based on how they live.

That is what it means to be under the law—to relate to God based on what we do, that our confidence before God is based on what we do, not based on what Jesus did and how God feels towards us. Being under the law means more than seeking to earn our salvation. It also means seeking to live rightly by the power of our own flesh. What I mean is by our own human resource, by our own human power, seeking to live godly. Now that we are born again, we know the only way to live godly is by interacting with the life of God that dwells in us; His name is the Holy Spirit. While we were under the law, we lived disconnected from God on the inside, simply because He did not live on the inside of us. We were living disconnected; the only power we had was our human ability.

In effect, Paul says, "You are not limited to your human ability anymore. You are not under the law anymore. You do not have to live disconnected from God on the inside because He lives in you, now that you are born again. You are under grace—you have power on the inside." Practically speaking, many, many believers, though they are under grace, live disconnected from God on the inside. They do not interact with the Holy Spirit on the inside of them, so basically they are living as though they are still under the law. They are living disconnected from God on the inside, and that is an implication of being under the law as well.

We Are Under Grace: The Implications of Being under Grace

To be under grace includes being enjoyed by God and empowered by the indwelling Spirit. We relate to God on the basis of what Jesus accomplished for us in His death and resurrection. It includes being under Jesus' generous and merciful leadership. We are under grace. Paul says it is just the opposite of being under the law. Now that you are born again, you are under grace. Again, being under grace has many implications.

Being under grace means that God enjoys the relationship; He actually enjoys us. I mean, can you imagine that God actually enjoys His relationship with you? We have this idea, when the enemy comes and lies to us, that God is on the verge of being finished with us. I tell you, it is not even close! He is not at all on the verge of being finished with you. That is an absolute lie, He actually enjoys the relationship, even though there are things that we do that grieve Him in the relationship, but He is committed to the relationship itself. He values it. He enjoys the interaction. We are His beloved children.

Being under grace also means that we are empowered by the indwelling Spirit. We have a resource on the inside that, if we interact with that Person, that resource, it will affect our mind and emotions. The taint of sin that is still on our mind and emotions—we can overpower it by that source on the inside. Being under grace also means we have a glorious new destiny.

Having Hope for the Future and being under Grace

One of the great pains of life common in the human race is people feeling they have no real future. When they think of their future, they feel like a failure. They have no hope for anything good happening towards them, and they feel like a failure in their life. They are not doing anything that actually really matters to anybody, their life is not making a difference at all, not really. They are putting a lot of energy into life, but they cannot see anything that really matters, that makes a difference. They do not see a good future. They know technically they go to heaven when they die, but they do not think much about it, so it mostly does not touch them.

Paul says, "You are under grace. You want to live in the reality of what you are under. You do not want to live disconnected from God on the inside or disconnected from your destiny in the future. You really do not want to live disconnected from those" (Rom. 6:11-14, paraphrased). Being under grace, we are under Jesus' generous and merciful leadership. Being under grace is being under Him, His Lordship. It is gracious. It is generous. It is kind. It is so patient—His generous leadership; that is the One we are under.

When we are under grace, we have confidence that we are loved. When we know we are under grace, when we are connected to the truth that God enjoys the relationship, that He actually enjoys us, when we have confidence that we are forgiven, then we have a new beginning every day. Is that not amazing? I can do something today that grieves the Spirit, and if I genuinely repent, I have a brand new day tomorrow. Every day is a new day. Every day really is. This lie that people have—I have gone too far, I am too messed up, I have sinned too often—it is over. Paul would say, "No, no, no, you are under grace! You have a new beginning every single day under His leadership. So do not live under this sense that it is hopeless, that it is too lost, that you failed too many times." He would say that it is just not true. We have the confidence that we can live differently. There are new possibilities. Internal righteousness and therefore external righteousness in our character is doable; it really is doable. Folks say, "Well, I have lived in so much lust for so many years as a believer, I do not really believe it is doable." Have you really embraced these three principles consistently in your life? Flawed and weak, but consistent? When you fail, do you sign back up to do them? "Well, technically no. I do not even know the three principles." Paul says that you have hope, it is doable, and it is within reach even for you.

Another thing about being in the grace of God is that from God's point of view, from His perspective in the most primary sense of the word, we are successful. From the biblical point of view, because God loves us, and we responded and love Him, we are already successful in the primary sense. The primary success of our life is already established in past tense. Now there is a secondary sense in which we want to be successful, and that is what we do outwardly, in the eyes of man. But in the primary sense, because God loves you and me, and we love Him—even though our love is weak and flawed, we love Him—we are successful.

Beloved, He sees our love is genuine. He sees it as real. God loves me; I love God—I am already successful in the primary sense. In the secondary sense we are still working in areas, but we can have that fundamental idea that we are not hopeless failures; we are not hopeless hypocrites; it is not all wasted. What we need to do is shift over to the grace paradigm of life and understand that we really are successful in God's sight already by virtue of the fact that He loves us and we are one of the minority of the human race who actually love Him.

There are 10 or 20 percent of us—some say 10 percent, some say 20 percent of the human race —that are saying yes to the grace of God. I do not really know the number, but it is still the minority of the human race. You have said yes to the grace of God. Beloved, you are already successful! I love to say that the thief on the cross, when he stepped over that line that day and entered paradise, he looked around and said, "Wow, if I had known I was a king, I never would have been a thief. I did not know. We do not have to wait until a day to figure out the truth about who we are.

Being under grace includes being enjoyed by God, indwelt by the Spirit, and empowered to live, and commissioned with a relevant purpose. We have received a new position, power, nature, insights, and destiny in Christ. Paul exhorted us to see ourselves as alive to God (v. 11); this means to live in the realm of God and grace. This includes cultivating a "grace paradigm" of our life. God sees our lives through the lens of grace, and therefore He sees it much differently than we do.

For example, all that we do in the will of God is rewarded because of grace or Jesus' generous evaluation of our lives—even our small deeds are remembered forever by God. (It is only because of grace that small acts such as giving someone a cup of water are rewarded). We need to cultivate a grace paradigm in our life perspective or paradigm. We need to see our lives through the lens of grace because that is how God sees our life. Beloved, we feel really different about ourselves, and we feel very different about our future, we feel different about our labors, and we feel different about our success when we have a grace paradigm—when we see ourselves in the way God sees us in Christ.

One of the Main Reasons Why Sincere Believers Quit Their Diligent Pursuit after Jesus.

Why do sincere believers quit in their diligent pursuit after Jesus? I mean they are pursuing Him diligently four or five years. They are going hard; they have a high vision. I have watched this for forty years. I mean, they are going hard five years, some for ten years, some less, some more, and the reason so many sincere believers give up is that sense of hopelessness. "I am not going to succeed anyway. I feel I am on the verge of being rejected by God. He is always mad at me anyway, why should I try? It is not going to work. Why should I put so much effort into the relationship when I keep failing, I keep stumbling in lust and bitterness and immorality? It is not going to happen anyway." Paul says, "Do not go there. Do not quit. You do not have to quit because the truth is you are under grace. God views your life in an entirely different way than you do by your natural thinking" (Rom. 6:14, paraphrased). Many people feel unnoticed by anybody. Nobody notices them in a positive way. They feel unappreciated. Life is hard, they put a lot of energy in it, and nobody believes in them. Nobody believes what they are doing matters. Nobody believes what they are doing is important. Nobody believes what they are doing is going to succeed. I think we underestimate the power of somebody believing in us. It is a very, very powerful reality when somebody that you value and somebody that you care about believes in you. Here is what I mean when I say that they believe in you—they believe you are genuine, they believe your efforts matter, they believe that what you do, though it is small, is important, they believe your future will succeed, and they believe that God is pleased with you. When somebody believes that about you, it is powerful, because in our own natural way we lose confidence in our own vision for our life. But when somebody we care about, who we value, speaks confidence over us, we go, "Wow!" Beloved, I have got good news for you. The One you love the most, who you care most about—Jesus—believes more about you than anybody else. This is called, "You are under the grace of God." It is a whole paradigm of life.

Jesus sees the genuineness of our weak love and desire to obey Him. He rejoices in our glorious future and destiny. He so values our small deeds and efforts. We are eternally fruitful. We are crowned with glory and honor (Heb. 2:7). We are successful in His eyes (all who love Jesus are already successful before God). Our life is no longer measured by what we achieve in man's eyes. We are His official ambassadors and are a part of the ruling class of the New Jerusalem. Paul addressed the common misinterpretation of the grace message (v. 15).

14. For sin shall not have dominion over you, for you are not under law but under grace. 15What then? Shall we sin because we are not under law but under grace? Certainly not! (Rom. 6:14-15)

1. **Grace empowers us to walk in a lifestyle of righteousness** and wholehearted obedience. As we see that we have freely received so much, we are overwhelmed with gratitude and come to understand our new position in Christ.

2. **Jesus redeemed us so that we would walk free from all sinful deeds** (Titus 2:14). He loves righteousness and is the most righteous man who ever lived.

14...who gave Himself for us, that He might redeem us from every lawless deed and purify for Himself His own special people, zealous for good works. (Titus 2:14)

3. **Being under His generous and merciful leadership** and living in deep relationship with Him will energize His people to wholehearted, obedient love. Paul gives the promise, and then he addresses a common misinterpretation that is often associated with biblical grace teaching.

He gives the promise in Romans 6:14. You do these three things, though weak and flawed. You embrace these three principles consistently, and Paul says, in effect, "I have got good news for you. Sin will not have dominion over your mind and emotions, your internal life. Therefore it will not have dominion over your external behavior. I promise you it will not in this age too, not just in the age to come.' Of course it will not in the age to come, but even in this age, sin will not have dominion over you. It is doable. It is within your reach. The man says, "Well, Paul, how could you say such a thing?"

Paul says, *"You are not under law."* You are not under condemnation. You no longer have to live disconnected from God. You are not powerless when those negative emotions rise up in you. You have a resource to challenge them. You have a future. You have no reason to be hopeless. God sees you as successful in the primary way, so there is no sense in quitting in despair. He enjoys the relationship, so no reason to give up. You are under grace. That is why I am telling you that this is going to work if you stay with it" (Rom. 6:14, paraphrased).

4. **Some completely misinterpret Paul's point** in emphasizing that we are not under the law. He is not saying that it does not matter how we live. Being free from the law does not invalidate the biblical moral standards in the kingdom because that would contradict the Sermon on the Mount. Unrighteousness is opposed to all that Jesus died for.

5. **Being free from the law is not a license for lawlessness.** Being under grace does not give us freedom to sin, but it gives us freedom from the

penalty of sin. Being under grace does not mean that we may continue in sin since we are not under sin's penalty.

6. **Grace does not condone sin**—it enables us to overcome sin. It is unthinkable to continue in willful sin for any who see their position as sons of God and as the Bride of Christ.

Rom. 6:15 is a very, very common error through Church history. It started in Paul's day. Some guy comes along and says, "Well, since we are under grace, since we are not under law but under grace, shall we keep sinning? Is it okay to be casual about sin because, I mean, if we are forgiven, why not keep sinning?" They completely misunderstand what Paul is arguing for, what he is presenting—the glorious vision he is putting in front of them. Paul says, "What?" He says, "No, no! You are forgiven to give you confidence to press in, to draw near, to enjoy the glory of this new partnership in righteousness with the heart of God.

Grace is not given to you so that because sin can be casual in your life. It is to give you confidence that righteousness is doable, that you have a new beginning everyday, that God is committed to you, that He enjoys the relationship. He believes in you" (Rom. 6:15). We believe in Him, but I am talking about in that sense I have just described as when somebody believes in you. What a glorious reality! Some people completely misinterpret what Paul is emphasizing here when he says that we are not under the law. They were doing it in Paul's day. It is no surprise that they have done it through Church history, and they are doing it today. Paul is the greatest grace preacher that ever walked the earth, and they did it to Paul. They rose up and they said,

"Wow, Paul, thank you! Since we are under grace, we are not under law, so it does not matter what we do." Paul says, "No, I am empowering you to be radical for righteousness, not to be casual about righteousness. What I am giving you is the exact opposite argument" (Rom. 6:15, paraphrased).

Paul is not saying it does not matter how we live. Being free from the law does not mean that the biblical standards, moral standards are now invalidated, that there is no purity, righteousness, truthfulness, humility in the kingdom. Paul is saying, "No, I am not invalidating the moral standards of God's kingdom. That would contradict the whole Sermon on the Mount" (Rom. 6:15, paraphrased).

Paul is not contradicting Jesus' teaching in the Sermon on the Mount. Paul repeated all of those spiritual values and moral values over and over through his teaching, and he associated it with the grace of God. What Paul wants them to know is that unrighteousness is a total contradiction to grace.

A casual attitude towards unrighteousness, and even a defeatist attitude that says, "I am never going to have victory anyway. It is not even doable," is a contradiction to the teaching of grace. Being free from law is not a license for lawlessness. Grace does not condone sin. Grace enables us to overcome sin by giving us confidence in a new being, a new power, and a new conversation on the inside—a new interaction with God Himself.

PRINCIPLE #1: Knowing the Truth (Faith).

Knowing Principle (Rom. 6:11): We must know who we are in Christ. To *"reckon ourselves"* alive to God is to see ourselves in the way that God sees us and to see what is true about our spirit because of being in Christ. Paul gives us details of our legal position (Rom. 6:1-10). 11Reckon [see] yourselves to be dead to sin, but alive to God in Christ... (Rom. 6:11)

Let's look at the three principles closer. Paul starts off, *"Reckon yourselves to be dead to sin and alive to God"* (Rom. 6:11). When he says, "Reckon yourselves," he is saying, "See yourself in the way God sees you in grace." It is essential that we know what we are supposed to know in the grace of God. It is essential that we know who we are in God's eyes. If we do not know how God sees us, we are never ever going to sustain our life in God. We are not going to sustain a life of victory or commitment against sin. We are going to just die in despair, emotionally I mean. We are going to cave, in despair. "It is not worth it anyway. It never works. God is mad. What is the use? It is all hopeless," that is how many people believe. The answer to those despairing, negative thoughts that are very, very common for sincere believers,

Paul gives in verse 11: Reckon yourself or see yourself through the lens of the grace of God.

Reckon yourself dead to sin: We are to see ourselves as dead to the reign of sin and thus finished with condemnation and powerlessness to challenge sinful promptings in our emotions.

Reckon yourself alive to God: We must see ourselves in the way that God sees us in Christ—as enjoyed, indwelt, empowered, and commissioned. To be alive to God is to live in the realm of God and of grace. When condemnation, shame, or lust rise up in us to challenge what God promised us, then we apply the promise of the Word by confessing the truth (Rom.10:8-10). Paul says that you are alive to God. What being alive to God means is that you live in the realm in which God lives. You live in the same realm that Jesus in His humanity lives in before the Father; you live in that realm. That is what it means to be alive to God. You live in the realm of God. You live in the realm of grace, You are not under the reign of sin; now you are in the reign of grace. Paul says that you have got to see it. Then, when negative emotions challenge the Word of God, you confess the Word, and you resist that negative mindset and those negative emotions.

PRINCIPLE #2: Resisting Darkness (Self-Denial in Choosing Godliness)

Resisting Principle (Rom. 6:12-13a): We resist sin, Satan, and sin-provoking circumstances. We can refuse to let sin reign in us by engaging in the three principles set forth in verse 11-13.

12. Therefore do not let sin reign in your mortal body, that you should obey it in its lusts. 13And do not present your members as instruments of unrighteousness to sin... (Rom. 6:12-13a)

The principles are very straightforward. They are not confusing. We just have to do them, and we have to do them consistently, even though we do them flawed and imperfectly. They still work if we do them consistently. They really, really do.

Principle number two: it is not enough that we know who we are in Christ. Biblical grace teaching involves more than knowing; it also involves resisting and pursuing. Some people present the teaching of grace only as knowing.

Paul is talking here about being under grace, and he gives all three principles. We cannot separate these three principles from Paul's grace teaching. If somebody does, it is a distorted grace message. <u>Therefore</u>: Paul wrote "therefore," pointing back to the truths of verses 1-11.

<u>Our members:</u> This speaks of our physical and mental capacities—our time, desires, speech, mind, emotions, or money. They can be used for good or evil. Our biblical view of grace and of holiness must incorporate verse 12-13. Paul said, *"Therefore, do not let sin reign in your body that you should obey its lusts" (Rom. 6:12)*. He goes on and adds a little bit more to the same principle, "Do not present your members as instruments of unrighteousness.

Do not present your members to sin" (Rom. 6:13). Paul uses this term, members, throughout Rom. 6. Now this idea of your members speaks of your physical and mental capacities and abilities. Your mental, your emotional, and your physical abilities and capacities are all incorporated as part of your members. So Paul uses the term, members, and he says, "Do not present, do not put your members—your mind, your thinking, your body—at the disposal of sin. Do not put it in the pathway of something that will stir sin up in your life. Do not do that" (Rom. 6:13, paraphrased). That is what he is saying here. In verse 12, he says, "Do not let sin reign in your body." The taint of sinful lusts, the taint of sin, is still on our mind and emotions as born-again believers who are new creations in Christ. Our born-again spirit has no sin in it at all. If your born-again spirit had sin in it, God the Holy Spirit could not dwell in you. God and sin cannot dwell together.

Your born-again spirit is where it is true of us to say that we are the righteousness of God in Christ Jesus. Our spirit man is strong, fully alive, and has the fullness of grace. It is our soul—our mind and emotions— that still has the taint of sin in it. Now Paul describes sin. He personifies sin. He describes sin like it is a king, like a person. He says, "Do not let King Sin make you obey because sin is going to try to get you to obey its lusts. I am telling you right now, you do not have to obey it. The lusts are still there. The taint is there, but you got a power within, and you have a new confidence because God enjoys the relationship. He has forgiven you. You feel good about your life, your destiny, your future because you are viewing your life through the lens of grace" (Rom. 6:121-14, paraphrased). So look at what he says in verse 12. He says, "Therefore." Now what is the therefore there for? Well it is referring to the verse before where he says, "See yourself alive to God," (verse 11), and in light of being of alive to God, living in the realm of God, being under grace, therefore you have the courage, the resolve, the confidence to say no to sin. He says, "When sin, that King Sin—those tainted emotions and feelings and those tainted mind and thoughts—comes against you, you have the authority to say, 'No, I am not going to yield to you'" (Rom. 6:12, paraphrased).

Paul's declaration here in verse 12 is that we can say no to sin. As a matter of fact we have to! Verse 12 is a strong exhortation that we have to engage our will; we have to make daily decisions to say no. Some people do not like that. They say, that's the downside. I mean, I just want God to do it for me." Jesus says, "No, I made provision so that when you do it, it works. I already made provision for you, but I am not going to do your part of the relationship, and you cannot do my part of the relationship."

So verse 12 is the biblical aspect. We must say no to sin. We must take a stand against sin, and we must deny it. Jesus will not deny sin for us in our daily life. Some people say, "Let the Lord do it." He says, "No, no, that is your part of the relationship. I have already made provision for you to have victory if you will do it." Others say, "Well, I am praying for a heavenly encounter, and if I get caught up in the third heavens, then I will not have deal with it." He says, "No, a heavenly encounter will not deal with it either." Remember, Paul had heavenly encounters, and he still had to say no to sin when it rose up in his members. Another guy says, "Well, let me go up front at the end of the meeting. Have them pray for me and cast it out." You can cast a demon out, but you cannot cast the taint the sin out of someone's mind and emotions. The way that we get victory—we renew our mind, we resist what we resist, we pursue God in the way verse 13 describes, and our sin does not have dominion. It does not have the upper hand in our thinking and our emotions. Over time we will experience that new liberty on the inside. Though the taint will be there, it will not have the upper hand. It will not be the dominant force it was before. It is our responsibility in the grace of God to refuse to allow sin to reign in us and to give our loving allegiance to Jesus. Denying our lustful desires is the theater God chose for us to express our love to Him. We do not earn God's love by obedience, but we express our love to God.

15. If you love Me, keep My commandments... (Jn. 14:15)

In the grace of God, it is our role in the relationship to choose not to allow sin to reign in us, but to give our loving allegiance to Jesus. One of the reasons why the Lord has made it a part the whole process of victory that we have to make this decision is that it is our way of expressing our love to Jesus. When we have negative emotions and a negative mindset, when they rise up in us, these negative feelings in our body, sinful feelings, and we say no to them because we love Him, He says, "I take that very personally. I know your "no" is weak, but I am moved by the fact that you love Me so much to say no." Now we do not earn the love of God by saying no, but, beloved, we express our love to God by saying no. Jesus said it Himself, "When you keep My commandments, you were demonstrating that you love Me and it moves Me. Even though your obedience is weak, it still moves Me. I take it very personally" (Jn. 14:15, paraphrased).

Do not let sin reign in your body: Not allowing sin to reign in us requires that we resist lust with self-denial and grace-empowered discipline. Grace motivates and empowers us to say no to sin. *11. The grace of God...has appeared to all men, 12. Teaching us that, denying ungodliness and worldly lusts, we should live soberly, righteously, and godly in the present age. (Titus 2:11-12)* 1. Jesus emphasized the need for self-denial (Mt. 16:24). The need for self-denial has been rejected or greatly minimized by many who promote a distorted grace message. *24"If anyone desires to come after Me, let him deny himself..."* (Mt. 16:24) 2. Paul needed to discipline his body by bringing it into subjection to Jesus (1 Cor. 9:27). *27I discipline my body and bring it into subjection lest...I should become disqualified. (1 Cor. 9:27)*

Do not let sin reign in your body (Rom. 6:12). Not allowing sin to reign requires self-denial. Look at Titus 2:11, "**The grace of God teaches us that we have to deny lust.**" The biblical grace teaching teaches us to deny lust. When we understand grace, we are so motivated with gratitude. We see our new potential because of the power of God in us. We see our new future. We have a new feeling about ourselves when we see ourselves in the grace of God. When we are listening to the grace of God from the biblical point of view, it will motivate us and energize us to deny ourselves when worldly lusts present themselves to us. Jesus emphasized denying self. He said, "Anyone who wants to follow Me—self-denial is a part of the relationship of loving Me" (Mt. 16:24).

In 1 Corinthians 9:27, Paul the apostle, the great grace teacher, the great teacher on the grace of God said, "I have to discipline my body." "Well, Paul, do you not understand grace? You are under grace." He says, "That is why I have the courage and the vision and the confidence to discipline myself. I know it is doable in the grace of God. I know who lives in me. I know who is looking at me. I know what my future is. I know how He evaluates me. I feel good about who I am in God, and, I tell you, I am motivated to discipline my body.

When those emotions rise up, those feelings, I bring my body in subjection to the Spirit lest I be disqualified." Now, this does not mean lest he be disqualified from salvation. He is not talking about losing his salvation here. He is talking about, lest he be disqualified from walking in the fullness of his apostolic ministry. He says, "I have to keep my body in subjection to the Spirit if I am going to walk out my apostolic calling. I absolutely have to do that" (1 Cor. 9:27, paraphrased).

Do not present your members to sin: People present themselves to sin in two stages—first in their mind, then with their body. We must refuse circumstances that inflame sinful desires. We do not go to places, buy items, look at, touch, or talk about that which stirs up sinful desires. Presenting ourselves to sin mentally: Presenting our members to sin starts in our mind by rehearsing different situations—by daydreaming. Jesus taught how immorality operates. It is rooted first in the mind, being fueled by sight. The progression of adultery begins with the mind and eyes, and moves to circumstances leading to physical adultery. *28*

Whoever looks at a woman to lust...has already committed adultery...in his heart (Mt. 5:28) 2. Presenting ourselves to s n physically: We must refuse circumstances that inflame sinful desires. We do not go to places, buy items, look at, touch, or talk about that which stirs up sinful desires. There are many ways to present oneself to sin. When the Bible tells us to not present our members to sin, this is very, very important. Paul says "Do not present your members"—your thinking, your emotions, your body—"Do not present your members to sin"—do not do it (Rom. 6:13, paraphrased). Now we present ourselves to sin when we fail in this. We present ourselves to sin in two stages. First, we present ourselves to sin in our mind through rehearsing scenes in our mind.

Past scenes, future scenes, potential scenes, we rehearse it in our mind; we call that daydreaming. But when we do that, beloved, we are actually presenting our members to the powerful fire of sinful desire. Paul says, "Do not present your members to that" (Rom. 6:13, paraphrased). Jesus taught on this principle too. So he is saying to avoid presenting your mind to sin. Do not present your physical person—do not go to the social event, do not look at things, do not buy things, do not have conversations, do not touch people in ways that stir you up. He is saying not to put yourself in a position where sin is inflamed in you.

PRINCIPLE #3: Pursuing God and People (Love)

Pursuing Principle (Rom. 6:13b): We pursue relating to and serving God and people with love. We present ourselves to God and our bodies as His instruments that He may use to bless others. In other words, we are to pursue loving God and people (Mt. 22:37-40). 13. *But present yourselves to God as being alive from the dead, and your members [your body, time, money, abilities, etc.] as instruments of righteousness to God. (Rom. 6:13b)*

Here is the third principle: pursuing God, pursuing people. It is a very simple principle. We know it well, so I am not going to mention here.

Present yourselves to God: This speaks of seeking to know, love, and please God in a personal and wholehearted way. We take time to cultivate intimacy with God. We present ourselves "as being alive from the dead" —or alive to God or with confidence in how God sees us in

Christ and based on what Jesus did for us, not based on our spiritual attainments, good or bad. Presenting ourselves with sincerity is not enough; we must have confidence in Jesus' work on the cross. **Present your members as instruments of righteousness:** We express love to people by offering ourselves to serve and bless others in God's will. This includes making the effort to be equipped to minister to others and to build quality relationships that glorify God.

We must know truth, resist darkness, and pursue God and people. We pursue loving God and people as we resist sin, Satan, and sin-provoking circumstances in the context of knowing who we are in Christ. None of these principles can be omitted. Some people resist sin and pursue God without knowing who they are in Christ. Some pursue God at prayer meetings without pursuing people or resisting sin. Others pursue people (relationship or ministry) without pursuing God. If we are going to walk in the victory that is promised to us, we must know truth of who we are in Christ. We must resist darkness—do not present your members to sin. And, we must pursue God. We have to know, we have to resist, and we have to pursue. We cannot do two out of the three and have the promise that sin will not have dominion in our mind and emotions. We have to do all three and do all three consistently, even though we do it in a weak and flawed way. That is just one little journey on this thing called victory over sin. We have a little bit more to go on this, but I just want to lay this out to you and put it before you. Amen and amen.

CHAPTER 6

THE SPIRIT OF ELIJAH AND DELIVERANCE FROM THE PRINCIPALITY OF JEZEBEL OVER CITIES

The ultimate blueprint for deliverance from the spirit of Jezebel lies within the scriptures. The spirit of Jezebel is more than sexual perversion. Sexual perversion is simply one of the outgrowths, leaves or physical signs that this powerful spiritual entity is in control in a particular region or nation in the earth. The Word of God and the biblical history of the nation of Israel is where the biblical personality, Jezebel, is first presented and it is where we are shown how Israel defeated this Queen from a heathen nation that had intermarried and intermingled with the kingdom of Israel, through her marriage to King Ahab in I Kings 16:31. If we can see how Israel defeated Jezebel, along with her false prophets and false gods of Baal, we can then know how to overcome the Jezebel spirit in our generation.

Though Jezebel was an actual biblical personality in scripture, as the Queen of King Ahab, the spirit of Jezebel represents and correlates in the New Testament scriptures to a false, illegitimate spiritual authority over regions or nations, called *Principalities,* that control national leaders, and their governing bodies, kings, and presidents, as well as religious, educational, and political institutions n cities and nations. This ruling spirit or principality influences laws, anc ungodly legislation that are passed in regions and nations bringing people under its sway and influence to perversion and dark spiritual forces. This term, Principality is found in the New Testament in Ephesians 6:12, saying, *for we wrestle not against flesh and blood, but against principalities, against powers, against the rulers of the darkness of this world, against spiritual wickedness in high places.*

The word *"Principality"* comes from the Greek word archē (ar-khay') which means; **a commencement, or (concrete) chief (in various applications of order, time, place or rank): - beginning, corner, (at the, the) first (estate), magistrate, power, principle, rule.**

This expression of the Jezebel spirit as a principality ruling over regions and nations, has the same aim that the biblical personality Jezebel had during her time in control over the nation of Israel. She wants to assume illegitimate authority and acceptance of her false gods and of her prophets to control the culture of the kingdom, or governing bodies where she attempts to rule. She did this in the Old Testament by way of manipulation, seduction and sorcery or witchcraft (2Kings 9:5). Once she manipulates and seduces the governing bodies or leadership over a region or nation, she then passes her laws, and establishes her word and will as the law of the land, and her prophetic voices and her gods as the gods over the region or land. Her gods are the idol gods of Baal that her father, Ethbaal served, the king of the Sidonians.

Jezebel's false gods of Baal

Baal was the name of the supreme god worshiped in ancient Canaan and Phoenicia. The practice of Baal worship infiltrated Jewish religious life during the time of the Judges (Judges 3:7), became widespread in Israel during the reign of Ahab (1 Kings 16:31-33) and also affected Judah (2 Chronicles 28:1-2). The word *"baal"* means "lord"; the plural is *baalim*. In general, Baal was a fertility god who was believed to enable the earth to produce crops and people to produce children. Different regions worshiped Baal in different ways, and Baal proved to be a highly adaptable god. Various locales emphasized one or another of his attributes and developed special "denominations" of Baalism. Baal of Peor (Numbers 25:3) and Baal-Berith (Judges 8:33) are two examples of such localized deities.

According to Canaanite mythology, Baal was the son of El, the chief god, and Asherah, the goddess of the sea. Baal was considered the most powerful of all gods, eclipsing El, who was seen as rather weak and ineffective. In various battles Baal defeated Yamm, the god of the sea, and Mot, the god of death and the underworld. Baal's sisters/consorts were Ashtoreth, a fertility goddess associated with the stars, and Anath, a goddess of love and war. The Canaanites worshiped Baal as the sun god and as the storm god—he is usually depicted holding a lightning bolt—who defeated enemies and produced crops. They also worshiped him as a fertility god who provided children. ***Baal worship was rooted in sensuality and involved ritualistic prostitution in the temples.*** At times, appeasing Baal required human sacrifice, usually the firstborn of the one making the sacrifice (Jeremiah 19:5). The priests of Baal appealed to their god in rites of wild abandon which included loud, ecstatic cries and self-inflicted injury (1Kings18:28).

Before the Hebrews entered the Promised Land, the Lord God warned against worshiping Canaan's gods (Deuteronomy 6:14-15), but Israel turned to idolatry anyway. During the reign of Ahab and Jezebel, at the height of Baal worship in Israel, God directly confronted the paganism through His prophet Elijah. First, God showed that He, not Baal, controlled the rain by sending a drought lasting three-and-one-half years (1 Kings 17:1). Then Elijah called for a showdown on Mt. Carmel to prove once and for all who the true God was. All day long, 450 prophets of Baal called on their god to send fire from heaven—surely an easy task for a god associated with lightning bolts—but "there was no response, no one answered, no one paid attention" (1 Kings 18:29). After Baal's prophets gave up, Elijah prayed a simple prayer, and God answered immediately with fire from heaven. The evidence was overwhelming, and the people "fell prostrate and cried, 'The LORD—he is God! The LORD—he is God!'" (verse 39)

This was Jezebels agenda in the nation of Israel when she married the King Ahab, the King of Israel, to set out to kill the prophets of Jehovah, and set up her prophets over the nation of Israel. After this she then established the gods of her people the Sidonians.

Elijah and the Defeat of Jezebel

Elijah (Hebrew: אֵלִיָּהוּ, *Eliyahu*, meaning "My God is Yahweh") was a prophet and a wonder-worker in the northern kingdom of Israel during the reign of Ahab (9th century BC), according to the biblical Books of Kings. According to the Books of Kings, Elijah defended the worship of Yahweh over that of the Canaanite god Baal; he raised the dead, brought fire down from the sky, and was taken up "by a whirlwind." (This means or mechanism of being taken up by a whirlwind is said plainly in 2 Kings chapter 2, first in verse 1 and then in verse 11, while the chariot and horses separated "the two of them," that is, Elijah and Elisha.) In the Book of Malachi, Elijah's return is prophesied "before the coming of the great and terrible day of the Lord," making him a harbinger of the Messiah. I believe that this prophesied return of Elijah before the coming of the day of the Lord could be speaking of the Church of the Living God, or God's house of Prayer for all nations, that will pray and shut up heaven that there will be no rain, and open the heavens to release rain, as was seen during Elijah's prophetic period (James 5:14-16).

In Judaism Elijah's name is invoked at the weekly Havdalah ritual that marks the end of Shabbat, and Elijah is invoked in other Jewish customs, among them the Passover seder and the Brit milah (ritual circumcision). He appears in numerous stories and references in the Haggadah and rabbinic literature, including the Babylonian Talmud.

In Christianity the New Testament describes how both Jesus and John the Baptist are compared with Elijah and on some occasions thought by some to be manifestations of Elijah, and Elijah appears with Moses during the Transfiguration of Jesus. Elijah is also a figure in various Christian folk traditions, often identified with earlier pagan thunder or sky gods. In the Qur'an and certain Islamic traditions, Elijah is described as a great and righteous man of God and one who powerfully preached against the worship of Ba'al.

Elijah shows us how to defeat the spirit of Jezebel with a prophetic word of the Lord, and specific, direct obedience to that word in 1st and 2nd Kings.

1Ki 19:15 And the LORD said unto him, Go, return on thy way to the wilderness of Damascus: and when thou comest, **anoint Hazael to be king over Syria:**

1Ki 19:16 **And Jehu the son of Nimshi shalt thou anoint to be king over Israel:** *and* **Elisha the son of Shaphat of Abelmeholah shalt thou anoint to be prophet in thy room.**

1Ki 19:17 And it shall come to pass, that him that escapeth the sword of Hazael shall Jehu slay: and him that escapeth from the sword of Jehu shall Elisha slay.

Overcoming the spirit of Jezebel

1Ki 19:18 Yet I have left me seven thousand in Israel, all the knees which have not bowed unto Baal, and every mouth which hath not kissed him.

These verses give specific detail of what's needed to defeat the spirit of Jezebel.

1. A National/Regional Prophet. v. 15 - **Elisha**
2. A Godly National/Regional Political Leader. v.16 - **Jehu**
3. A Pure people of Prayer that have not bowed to Baal (Idols, Jezebel's political and religious system) v.18; 2 Ki 9:32 – **Eunuchs**.

A Testimony of the Process of raising up Political Jehu's to Defeat Jezebels

One day while I was reading 2nd Kings 9, which deals with the Prophet Elijah's directive for one of his sons to go and anoint Jehu as the next king of Israel, God spoke to my heart that He was going to have me to anoint the next Mayor of my city of Columbus Ohio, with the Spirit of Jehu, to bring down the spirit of Jezebel over the city.

2Ki 9:1 *Then Elisha the prophet called one of the sons of the prophets and said to him, "Tie up your garments, and take this flask of oil in your hand, and go to Ramoth-gilead. 2 And when you arrive, look there for Jehu the son of Jehoshaphat, son of Nimshi. And go in and have him rise from among his fellows, and lead him to an inner chamber. 3 Then take the flask of oil and pour it on his head and say, 'Thus says the LORD, I anoint you king over Israel.' Then open the door and flee; do not linger."*

As I read these verses and heard that directive from the Holy Spirit, my immediate response was, that I don't know anybody that's running for Mayor. But I felt the persistence of the Holy Spirit and the assurance of God that He would connect me with those that would be candidates for Mayor in my city real soon. It wasn't a few days afterwards, that the standing Mayor who had been the Mayor for the last 16 years, announced that he would not be running for another term as mayor in the upcoming election cycle, which would be the in fall of that year. SO there would be a primary run-off to determine who would be the candidates on the ticket for the fall elections, and they would begin with the next 30 days. And not only did God do what he said he would do, to connect me with two mayoral candidates in my city, but He brought me into direct contact with a Presidential Candidate, and with a whole party convention head, with access to the various political candidates for President all within two months. It only took about two weeks before I was introduced firstly to two Mayoral candidates in our City. In the first instance, two weeks later, I was texted an invitation to a particular candidacy announcement at the King Arts Center in my city. At first, I did not respond to this invitation, totally forgetting about the previous two weeks dialogue with the Holy Spirit around 2 Kings 9:2, because I had a previously scheduled appointment on that same date. But God is patient with us, the text came again, with the sender being very persistence, stating she really felt like I was supposed to be there. At that moment it hit me, that this was the fulfilment of that promise God had made to me, that he would connect me with a candidate for Mayor real soon. I immediately texted back, my confirmation that I would be there.

On the day of the candidacy announcement, I arrived at the place where there where many dignitaries and public officials in our city that were in attendance to hear the candidates announce6ment. As I mingled amongst the dignitaries, I realized the enormity of my task, and wondered how and what God wanted me to do. It just seemed so out of synch with the flow of the night, for me just to interrupt the proceedings and walk up to the candidate and attempt to anoint him with the spirit of Jehu to be the next mayor of Columbus. As I began to rationalize why it was out of order to attempt such an act, one of the organizers of the night came up to me and asked, "Are you Pastor Mathis?" I said, "Yes, I am." And then he replies, "We have you on the program to open up in prayer, and we're about to get started with the program in about 5 minutes. He went on to say, "I will call you up first for your prayer and then we will go from there." I said, yes and then I turned my attention to the Lord, knowing that he had just done away with my excuse and issue of not being in the flow with the program and in synch with the night. Now I was not only in the flow and synch with the program, I was opening up the program with prayer. The very thing God told me to do over this candidate about three weeks prior.

Overcoming the spirit of Jezebel

As the organizer and emcee called me up, I brought my bible with me, bookmarked to 2 Kings 9. As I approached the microphone, I began by addressing the candidate, who was to the right of the room, by saying, Sir, I do not know you, nor have I ever heard of you, But I got a scripture a few weeks ago, to pray over the next Mayor over our city, anointing him with the Spirit of Jehu, to bring down the spirit of Jezebel over our city., so if you want to be the next mayor of our city, I have to pray this over you. Just to give a little context to this story, our city had been run for the past 16 years, by one of the most liberal Mayors of our nation. He was not only a proponent of the emerging lifestyle of Homosexuality and Lesbianism, he was on record as saying that it was his aim to make Columbus Ohio the most gay friendliest city in our nation. Columbus Ohio at this point had the second highest gay and lesbian community in the nation, behind only San Francisco.

As I made this statement to this Mayoral candidate, I then told him and the audience of dignitaries, that I was simply going to read the verses from second Kings and then pray it over him. So I read the below verses, and begin to pray and anoint him with the spirit of Jehu to be the next Mayor of Columbus Ohio.

2Ki 9:6 So he arose and went into the house. And the young man poured the oil on his head, saying to him, "Thus says the LORD, the God of Israel, I anoint you king over the people of the LORD, over Israel.

2Ki 9:7 And you shall strike down the house of Ahab your master, so that I may avenge on Jezebel the blood of my servants the prophets, and the blood of all the servants of the LORD.

2Ki 9:8 For the whole house of Ahab shall perish, and I will cut off from Ahab every male, bond or free, in Israel.

I THEN PRAYED: In the name of Jesus, I anoint you with favor and with power, with the Spirit of Jehu, to bring down Jezebel over our City. I declare, should you become the next mayor of our city, you shall establish godliness and righteousness as the banner over our city.

Afterwards everybody in the room began to excitedly and enthusiastically applaud for about two minutes. Once he came up to make his announcement he had tears in his eyes as he began his prepared statement of announcement.

Two weeks later, a second candidate for mayor was invited, unbeknownst to me, to the weekly pastoral fellowship luncheon I attend in my city. He was there to address the Pastors and get their backing for his soon coming candidacy for Mayor. He was presently the standing Sheriff of the city and he was a believer in Jesus. After he finished his address of the pastors, he opened up the floor for questions. Of course, my first question was, "where do stand on gay marriage and homosexuals and lesbians desire to re-define marriage. The next 45 minutes was a lively discussion as he stated his Christian beliefs about marriage being the union between one man with one woman. He discussed his non-discriminatory philosophy concerning homosexuals.

To give further context, in our city of Columbus Ohio, the past Mayor, in his attempt to make our city the most gay friendly city in our nation, had appointed a lesbian chief of police, He had appointed a Homosexual Board of Education President, and in the schools, this president of the board of education had appointed majority gay and lesbian principals over the public schools, and established a gay pride week in all of the public schools. So we had a lively discussion that day, about how we can stem the tide of Jezebel over our city. Afterwards, all the Pastors prayed over this second candidate, that should he be the next mayor of our city, he would have the spirit of Jehu to bring down the spirit of Jezebel over our city. Two weeks later both of these candidates for mayor were a part of a 4 man race for the top two spots for the fall elections. In the primary of the top four, the standing Mayor's endorsed candidate won the top spot and a place on the ticket for his party, and the other two candidates that God had enabled me to release the spirit of Jehu over, ended up tied for second, and needed a recount to determine who would get the last spot in the fall elections.

Overcoming the spirit of Jezebel

A Divine Connection with a Presidential Candidate for the Jehu Prayer

In the midst of all of this, while on my way home from a speaking engagement in Pittsburg Pennsylvania, as I was boarding the plane, I ran into Ben Carson, an African-American candidate for President of the United States, who had just put his name in the race that week. As I got on the plane with him, I introduced myself to h m, and told him, I felt like I was supposed to pray for him and bless his candidacy and campaign. He obliged me, I was released a blessing and the power of Jehu over his life and campaign. Later in the fl ght, I was able to give him a signed copy of one of my books and leave the Aaronic Blessing in the front cover. And lastly, I was able to take a picture with him as we got off the plane.

Jehu represents the political/governmental leadership over countries and regions that must be in place to establish godliness, righteousness and peace and bring down Jezebel. In order for the principality of Jezebel to be brought down it takes a Prophet of God with the spirit of Elijah on them, it takes a godly King, President or Prime minister, with the spirit of Jehu on him, and it takes a godly priesthood with a Eunuch anointing and a spirit of purity on them.

2Ki 9:22 And when Joram saw Jehu, he said, "Is it peace, Jehu?" He answered, <u>"What peace can there be, so long as the whorings and the sorceries of your mother Jezebel are so many?"</u>

2Ki 9:23 Then Joram reined about and fled, saying to Ahaziah, "Treachery, O Ahaziah!"

2Ki 9:24 And Jehu drew his bow with his full strength, and shot Joram between the shoulders, so that the arrow pierced his heart, and he sank in his chariot.

2Ki 9:25 Jehu said to Bidkar his aide, "Take him up and throw him on the plot of ground belonging to Naboth the Jezreelite. For remember, when you and I rode side by side behind Ahab his father, how the LORD made this pronouncement against him:

Once Jehu was anointed by the prophet, he was empowered to take down the prince–a-pality that had been ruling over the nation, through the many whorings, and sorceries of Jezebel. Notice Jehu says, what peace can there be as long as the whoring and sorceries of your mother Jezebel ARE SO MANY. Jezebel has many perverted sexual expressions by which she disturbs the peace of whole cities. And until the spirit or principality of Jezebel is dealt with there can be no peace in a city. After the king or ruling leadership influenced by Jezebel is removed, then you can deal with Jezebel herself, or you can deal with the perversion and the spirit of perversion that is released by Jezebel through the establishing and worship of her false deity "Baal." After Jehu had killed the standing King that was allowing Jezebel to set up her gods of sexual immorality and perversion, he then went after Jezebel herself.

2Ki 9:30 When Jehu came to Jezreel, Jezebel heard of it. And she painted her eyes and adorned her head and looked out of the window.

2Ki 9:31 And as Jehu entered the gate, she said, "Is it peace, you Zimri, murderer of your master?"

2Ki 9:32 <u>And he lifted up his face to the window and said, "Who is on my side? Who?" Two or three eunuchs looked out at him</u>.

2Ki 9:33 He said, "Throw her down." So they threw her down. And some of her blood spattered on the wall and on the horses, and they trampled on her.

The Eunuch Anointing and the Defeat of Jezebel

Once the kingly leadership is removed and replaced with a godly King or governmental leader, you then have to have a partnership established with those that are called and separated to the Lord in his house. In 2 Kings 9:32, Jehu did not directly kill Jezebel, but in partnership with the two eunuchs, which represents the present and emerging prayer movement, with day and night prayer and worship by those that are called and set-apart by God to His house of prayer. These in the house of prayer, called to keep the fire of the altar burning, are the Eunuchs on the Lord's side that will throw down the spirit of Jezebel over regions, in partnership with the Kings wishes and command to *THROW HER DOWN*.

In order to defeat Jezebel you need a Prophet, you need a King, and you need a Eunuch that has separated himself to God in God's House of Prayer. The house of prayer model of the expression of the End of Days Church to overthrow the spirit of Jezebel with the Eunuchs anointing is the principle weapon in this battle seen in Isaiah 56:6-9

Isa 56:4 <u>For thus says the LORD unto the eunuchs that keep my Sabbaths, and choose the things that please me, and take hold of my covenant;</u>

Isa 56:5 Even unto them will I give in mine house and within my walls a place and a name better than of sons and of daughters: I will give them an everlasting name, that shall not be cut off.

Isa 56:6 Also the sons of the stranger, that join themselves to the LORD, to serve him, and to love the name of the LORD, to be his servants, every one that keeps the Sabbath from polluting it, and taketh hold of my covenant;

Isa 56:7 <u>Even them will I bring to my holy mountain, and make them joyful in my house of prayer: their burnt offerings and their sacrifices shall be accepted upon mine altar; for mine house shall be called an house of prayer for all people.</u>

The Building of God's House to Overthrow Jezebel's House

This house that will establish the Eunuch anointing to overthrow the Jezebel spirit is actually the house that David built. David shows us how to overthrow the spirit of Jezebel with worship and prayer day and night to release victories over principalities over whole regions.

As a young man David showed how to defeat giants over regions through worship when He defeated Goliath as a 17 year old boy in the valley of Elah. I believe David's victory of Goliath in I Samuel 17 is also a picture how to cast down principalities over whole regions with the spirit of the tabernacle of David. The spirit of the tabernacle of David was initiated in the sheepfold as he worshipped while watching over his father's sheep. It was during these times that David learned the presence of God that comes from the place of worship and how to hear

God's voice and commune with him from that place of worship. It was also during these times of relational interaction with Jehovah God that David experienced victories over the bear and the lion that came into the fold to take a lamb from his father's flock that caused him to understand the power of his covenant keeping God. Therefore, we can see David's process that ultimately led him to defeat Goliath. If Goliath is symbolic in the spirit realm of principalities that hold whole regions in fear and bondage, we can see through David how to defeat these principalities over our cities, nations, and regions.

The Process of Defeating Principalities

Most casual readers of David's victory over Goliath go directly to the valley of Elah and focus on the 5 smooth stones that David picked up to place in his sling shot to hurl at Goliaths head. However, David's victory did not begin in the valley, it began in the sheepfold feeding his father's sheep in Bethlehem. It was there in the sheepfold of Bethlehem feeding his father's flock, playing on his harp and worshipping Jehovah that David established a succession of victories over lions and bears that attempted to ravage his father's flock that gave David the courage to face Goliath and defeat Israel's greatest enemy.

1Sa 17:34 And David said unto Saul, Thy servant kept his father's sheep, and there came a lion, and a bear, and took a lamb out of the flock:

1Sa 17:35 And I went out after him, and smote him, and delivered it out of his mouth: and when he arose against me, I caught him by his beard, and smote him, and slew him.

1Sa 17:36 Thy servant slew both the lion and the bear: and this uncircumcised Philistine shall be as one of them, seeing he hath defied the armies of the living God.

1Sa 17:37 David said moreover, The LORD that delivered me out of the paw of the lion, and out of the paw of the bear, he will deliver me out of the hand of this Philistine. And Saul said unto David, Go, and the LORD be with thee.

The first process of David's defeat of the principality of Goliath was his fearlessness turned to faith in his covenant keeping God through worship. Principalities rule by fear and deception, but Jesus rules through love and worship or intimacy. Goliath presented himself for 40 days in Socoh, and stood and shouted to the ranks of Israel;

I Sam. 17:8 Why are ye come out to set your battle in array? am not I a Philistine, and ye servants to Saul? choose you a man for you, and let him come down to me.

9 If he be able to fight with me, and to kill me, then will we be your servants: but if I prevail against him, and kill him, then shall ye be our servants, and serve us.

10 <u>And the Philistine said, I defy the armies of Israel this day; give me a man, that we may fight together.</u>

11 <u>When Saul and all Israel heard those words of the Philistine, they were dismayed, and greatly afraid.</u>

The armies of Saul heard this for 40 days continually, building in them day by day the fear and the dread for Goliath. However, David was not in Socoh hearing Goliath's threats and taunts for those 40 days, David was in the flock with his father's sheep, worshipping and establishing experiences with his covenant keeping God. So when David came and heard Goliath's threats and taunts he was full of the faith of his God, not the fear of Goliath.

1Sa 17:14 And David was the youngest: and the three eldest followed Saul. 15 <u>But David went and returned from Saul to feed his father's sheep at Bethlehem. 16 And the Philistine drew near morning and evening, and presented himself forty days.</u>

David therefore was spending his time feeding his earthly father's sheep instead of listening to the taunts of the principality over that region. The process of feeding the sheep of God, along with worship and prayer, I believe, is the first steps in defeating the principality over regions. We can either listen to the taunts of the enemy or we can listen to and obey the voice and will of the father. If we are faithful to the will of the father to feed His sheep I believe God will be faithful to his covenant to impart into us his covenant faithfulness.

1Sa 17:19 Now Saul, and they, and all the men of Israel, were in the valley of Elah, fighting with the Philistines.

20 <u>And David rose up early in the morning, and left the sheep with a keeper, and took, and went, as Jesse had commanded him; and he came to the trench, as the host was going forth to the fight, and shouted for the battle.</u>

21 For Israel and the Philistines had put the battle in array, army against army. 22 <u>And David left his carriage in the hand of the keeper of the carriage, and ran into the army, and came and saluted his brethren.</u>

23 And as he talked with them, <u>behold, there came up the champion, the Philistine of Gath, Goliath by name, out of the armies of the Philistines, and spoke according to the same words: and David heard them.</u>

24 And all the men of Israel, when they saw the man, fled from him, and were sore afraid.

26 And David spoke to the men that stood by him, saying, What shall be done to the man that kills this Philistine, and taketh away the reproach from Israel? <u>for who is this uncircumcised Philistine, that he should defy the armies of the living God?</u>

27 And the people answered him after this manner, saying, so shall it be done to the man that kills him.

David went on to defeat this giant Goliath, establishing victory in the whole region and obtaining favor in King Saul's court to become Saul's armor bearer. David's worship and prayer model from the time of feeding his father's flock had taken him from the sheepfold and the victories over bears and lions, to a major victory over the rulers over Israel in the land, on unto the Kings court of Saul and eventually the throne of Israel as King of all of Israel. What was the key to David's success in battle? David was a worshipper, David was faithful, David was a servant and David was courageous. He knew that God was with him.

David's Vow to Build a Place for God's Presence

As a young man, David made a vow to dedicate his life to find a resting-place or dwelling place for God. This refers to a place where an unusual measure of God's presence is manifest on earth. David's life work was to establish a dwelling place for God in Jerusalem in his generation.

> *1 LORD, remember David and all his afflictions; 2 How he swore to the LORD, and vowed to the Mighty One: 3 "Surely I will not go into the chamber of my house, or go up to the comfort of my bed; 4 I will not give sleep to my eyes...5 until I find a place for the LORD, a dwelling place for the Mighty One of Jacob"...8 Arise, O, Lord, to Your resting place. (Ps. 132:1-8)*

David vowed to live in extravagant devotion to seek the Lord with all his resources (time, talents, treasures). His vow included spending time in God's House (Ps. 27:4), fasting (Ps. 69:7-12), extravagant giving of his money (1 Chr. 22:14) and embracing God's order in worship. This vow changed history and continues today in those who embrace it. It is at the heart of the End-Time worship movement. The Lord, will raise up a million believers who fully walk out this vow. David's vow positioned his heart to receive insight into the worship that God seeks.

> *23 True worshipers will worship the Father in spirit and truth; for the Father is seeking such to worship Him. (Jn. 4:23)*

David received revelation of worship in God's heavenly sanctuary (1 Chr. 28:11-19).

> *96 I have seen the consummation of all perfection (God's Throne of Glory)... (Ps. 119:96.) 11. David gave his son Solomon the plans...12 for all that he had by the Spirit, of the courts of the house of the LORD...13 also for the division of the priests and the Levites, for all the*

> work of the service of the house of the LORD...19 All this," said David, "the LORD made me understand in writing, by His hand upon me, all the works of these plans." (1 Chr. 28:11-19)
>
> 2 I heard a voice from heaven, like the voice of many waters, and...loud thunder. I heard the sound of harpists...3 They sang...a new song before the Throne... (Rev. 14:2-3)
>
> 13 Every creature which is in heaven and on the earth...saying: "Blessing and honor...be to Him who sits on the Throne, and to the Lamb, forever and ever!" 14 The twenty-four elders fell down and worshiped Him who lives forever and ever. (Rev. 5:13-14)

The KJV says that God "inhabits (lives in or manifests His life) in the praise of His people. David taught that when we sing praise that God inhabits (manifests His power) in that context. 3. You are...enthroned (manifest the power of Your Throne) in the praises of Israel. (Ps. 22:3)

David's revelation of heavenly worship (as seen in Psalms) is foundational to David's throne which is "political government in the spirit of the Tabernacle of David" or government based on 24/7 worship and intercession. David's government flowed forth from prophetic worship (1 Chr. 23-25). David had revelation of the spiritual impact of prophetic intercessory worship (Ps. 22:3).

> 6 Let the high praises of God be in their mouth... 7 to execute vengeance (justice) on the nations, and punishments on the peoples; 8 to bind their kings with chains...9 to execute on them the written judgment-- this honor have all His saints. (Ps. 149:6-9)

After David became king, the first thing he did was to capture Jerusalem (2 Sam. 5:3-10). Then he gave expression to his sacred vow by setting up a worship tabernacle in Jerusalem (2 Sam. 6). David received revelation from God about establishing God's order of worship first in Jerusalem. One of the first things that Jesus will do when He rules Jerusalem is to establish worship there.

> 1 David...prepared a place for the ark of God, and pitched a tent for it...16 David spoke to the...Levites to appoint...singers accompanied by instruments of music... (1 Chr. 15:1-16)

David put Levites before the Ark (which spoke of God's Throne and presence) to worship God.

> 1 They brought the ark...and set it in the midst of the tabernacle that David erected for it. 4 He appointed Levites (singers) to minister before the ark...to praise the Lord...37 to minister before the ark regularly, as every day's work required... (1 Chr. 16:1, 4, 37)

David established 4,000 full-time paid musicians, 288 singers (12 x 24 = 288) and 4,000 gatekeepers.

> 7 The number...instructed in the songs of the Lord...who were skillful, was 288. (1 Chr. 25:7) 4,000 were gatekeepers, and 4,000 praised the Lord with musical instruments... (1 Chr. 23:5)

David commanded God's people to honor the heavenly order of worship that he received by revelation because it was God's command (2 Chr. 29:25; 35:4, 15; Ezra 3:10; Neh. 12:45). These worship principles are timeless and valid today, such as establishing singers and musicians in God's House. The application of these principles would differ in each generation and culture.

> 25 Hezekiah...stationed Levites in the house of the Lord with stringed instruments... according to the commandment of David...for thus was the commandment of the Lord.(2 Chr. 29:25)

David provided financial support so that singers could sing as a full-time occupation.

> *33 These are the singers...who lodged in the chambers, and were free from other duties; for they were employed in that work day and night. (1 Chr. 9:33)*

God's order for supporting the singers and gatekeepers was revealed to David. The storehouse was the central place to receive tithes that was under the spiritual leadership of the Lord's House. Asaph and his brothers were included in the 288 singers (12 x 24 = 288).

> *37 So he left Asaph and his brothers there before the ark of the covenant of the LORD to minister before the ark regularly, as every day's work required... (1 Chr. 16:37)*

David gave over $100 billion (according to today's prices) to God's House from his personal finances. One talent equals about 75 lbs or 1200 ounces (16 ounces in a pound). 100,000 talents weighed about 7.5 million pounds (almost 4,000 tons). At $700 an ounce, a talent of gold would be worth about $850,000. Thus, 100,000 talents of gold would be worth about $85 billion. A talent of silver at $12 an ounce is worth nearly $15,000, thus one million talents of silver (75 million pounds or almost 40,000 tons) is worth about $15 billion.

> *1 Indeed I have taken much trouble to prepare for the House of the LORD 100,000talents of gold ($85 billion) and 1,000,000 talents of silver ($15 billion)... (1 Chr. 22:14)*

A Prophet, King and a Priest that won't Bow

Once you get a Prophet with the Spirit of Elijah, and you get a king with an anointing to stand up to the spirit of Jezebel and not give in to her whoredoms or her sorcery, decreeing and standing on the side of God's laws, you then need a house of eunuchs, a house of prayer that will throw her down in prayer from her high place over a region or nation. This is what God is getting ready to raise up from the Church that has come out from her influence and from her harlot Babylon system - *A Prophet in the spirit of the Elijah, a King in the spirit of Jehu, and a Davidic Priesthood after the order of Melchizedek, a company of Eunuchs that will set themselves apart from the world, the religious system and will enter into a consecration that will take on and thrown down Jezebels influence in the nations of the earth.*

In order for the Church to be positioned to arise from her current place and come into this new position of power and influence over Jezebel in the nations, we have to come off of a depencency on her gods for pleasure and perverted and sensual sexuality - Baal. We must come off of a dependency upon her system of operation, living by her resources and provision.

The reason Elijah was able to confront Jezebel was because he had not bowed down to Baal (I Kings 17, 18) His pleasure was found in doing the will of God, and speaking the word of God. He had an allegiance to Jehovah and His system of operation and provision found in the house of prayer in the presence of God. If you are living dependent upon Jezebel's system, if you're living by the word from Jezebel's prophets, and if you are living off of Jezebel's provision and prosperity, eating from her table, you will be influenced by Jezebel's spirit of immorality, manipulation and witchcraft. And you will eventually bow down to the spirit of Baal, which is Jezebel's god of sexual fertility and perverse sexuality. Many in the body of Christ that name the name of Christ are struggling with the spirit of immorality and sexual perversion, not because they don't have a heart after God, nor because they just aren't sincere in their desire after the ways and will of God, but because they are tied into Jezebel's religious system. They are tied into the spirit and system of the world, *which is the lust of the flesh, the lust of the eyes and the pride of life* (1 John 2:16). They are living motivated and directed by the culture, and not the kingdom. They are living by the world and not by the word of God.

The Spirit of Moses and Elijah on the End-Time Praying Church

The picture we will get and the impartation we will receive from the end-time praying church will cause us to rise up be like Moses in Egypt and Elijah in Israel. We will have the spirit of confrontation to deal with sin, sickness, and evil, as well as an ungodly church and political system that will be challenged by the end time prayer movement. As they were in the prayer movements seen both in Moses' day in Egypt and in Elijah's day in Israel, the end-time church is going to have power to confront sin and Satan himself. As Elijah on Mt Carmel, challenging the ungodly, wicked, religious system in Israel of the prophets of Baal, and as Moses in Egypt challenging Pharaoh's system of oppression and slavery, the spirit of the Prophets Moses and Elijah will come on the end-time praying church. It will come on the Church for the operation of the prophetic that we will see released and raised up in the church. This Spirit will return His church to a House of Prayer, releasing the judgments on the religious and political systems of these last days. This prophetic spirit of Moses and Elijah that is coming on the end-time prayer movement in His house of prayer is going to be the spirit that prepares the church to confront the Anti-Christ system of the last days and stand in the face of persecution and death unflinching and unrelenting, releasing the end-time Judgments on the world recorded in the book of the Revelation. The Church does not have this end-time spirit yet because we have not yet come out of Jezebel's religious and political system. But this is what's coming in the last days at the End of the Age, with the End of Days Church.

CHAPTER 7

OVERCOMING SEXUAL PERVERSION BY GODS LOVE AND LAW

Mat 5:27 You have heard that it was said by them of old time, Thou shalt not commit adultery: 8 But I say unto you, That whosoever looks on a woman to lust after her hath committed adultery with her already in his heart.

In this chapter I want to address Matthew 5:27, 30, where Jesus calls His disciples to overcome the spirit of immorality. I believe that when Jesus gave this message He was speaking in a very tender way. Why? Because He desires to help the ones He loves. One of the main deceptions of Jezebel in this generation of immorality, especially as related to Homosexuals and Lesbians is the love verses intolerance message. Many well-meaning people, Christians and non-Christians alike, use the deceptive message of the Love of God confusing God's love with the emotional, lust-filled expression of Love we've come to know as love in this present generation.

Here's why I say that: sometimes we have this false dichotomy between tender or Loving and bold. If we're tender we lower the standards and say, "Ah, gee, we understand." If we're bold, we say, "Get with it!" So boldness sometimes goes with being harsh, and tenderness goes with compromise. No. We don't have to pick between the two. We can be bold and tender and uncompromising in this message about overcoming immorality, because it's really a message about love, not hate or condemnation. Jesus' message to the woman caught in adultery was both stern and loving. He could have condemned her to death for being caught in the act of Adultery, but he refused to condemn her, but at the same time that He liberated her from her death sentence at the hands of the religious Pharisees, he then told her, GO AND SIN NO MORE.

Joh 8:2 Early in the morning he came again to the temple. All the people came to him, and he sat down and taught them. 3 The scribes and the Pharisees brought a woman who had been caught in adultery, and placing her in the midst 4 they said to him, "Teacher, this woman has been caught in the act of adultery. 5 Now in the Law Moses commanded us to stone such women. So what do you say?" 6 This they said to test him, that they might have some charge to bring against him. Jesus bent down and wrote with his finger on the ground. 7 And as they continued to ask him, he stood up and said to them, "Let him who is without sin among you be the first to throw a stone at her." 8 And once more he bent down and wrote on the ground. 9 But when they heard it, they went away one by one, beginning with the older ones, and Jesus was left alone with the woman standing before him. 10 Jesus stood up and said to her, "Woman, where are they? Has no one condemned you?"11 She said, "No one, Lord." And Jesus said, "Neither do I condemn you; go, and from now on sin no more."

How could Jesus expect this woman to just stop her adultery at His command to *SIN NO MORE*? No doubt this was not this woman's first incidence with sexual immorality. Furthermore, if the threat of death by stoning wasn't enough to curb her appetites, dictates and desires for sex outside of marriage, how would five short words – GO AND SIN NO MORE - empower her to leave that lifestyle. I believe it was the Love of God that Jesus showed this woman in not condemning her, but being willing to protect, cover and tenderly instruct her in Love, how to be free from the condemnation of sin and immorality, as well as how to be free from the Jezebel expression of Adultery, that empowered her to turn away from the lifestyle of Adultery, Jesus did not excuse or explain away her sin by giving her allowance to commit adultery by finding some loop hole in the law to justify Him not allowing her to be stoned.

He did not argue for her innocence with the Pharisees to keep them from stoning her to death. No! Jesus exposed the sin in all of humanity. At the heart of all encounters with sexual immorality, both heterosexual and homosexual, is the problem of our human nature. WE WERE ALL BORN THIS WAY! We were born in sin with the propensity to pursue any and every vile addiction that would be presented to us by God's arch-enemy, Satan, to mock God. Knowing that we were all born in sin and shaped in iniquity (Psalm 51:5), Jesus chose to be Her savior rather than her Judge, because that's what He came for - *to save us from our sins* - not to zap us because of our sins. So when the firing squad was set to execute her by stoning, he would only allow the ones who had never sinned to participate in her judgment and execution. This disqualified the whole firing squad from participating in her death by stoning. There was only one standing there that had no sin - Jesus Himself - and He chose to die for her sin instead of requiring her to die for her own sin by stoning. I believe the power to SIN NO MORE, was in His love to deliver her from the penalty of sin - death. Onc3.e He revealed to her that he came that she might have life and not death, when death was what the law required for sin (Romans 8:1), I believe she was empowered by His love to SIN NO MORE. When we truly show the love of Christ, as Christians, to those that are trapped by the spirit of Jezebel in sexual immorality, we will not leave people in compromise with sin, nor will we leave them hiding from their sins in the church behind their religious pretense and titles like the Pharisees. But we will love them out of their struggle with sin, knowing that Jesus died in our place, and but for the grace of God, there go I.

Love Follows Jesus out of sin all the way to the Cross

This woman, caught in Adultery, yet loved out of the consequence of her sin by the light of Christs' words (John 8:12), would be one of only three followers of Jesus at the foot of the cross when Jesus was crucified. Of all His twelve disciples, of all the 70 disciples in Luke 10, and of all the thousands he fed and ministered to during His earthly ministry, she was one of only three to stay with Him all the way to the cross. She was not afraid to be seen with Him, a convicted criminal, nor was she afraid that she would be crucified by association, as many of the His disciples were afraid of. And it's interesting to note that the other two, John the Beloved, and Mary the mother of Jesus, both had an intense love of Jesus, and knew beyond a shadow of a doubt that Jesus loved them. Love doesn't leave a person in sin and compromise with immorality. Love tenderly delivers a person from sin by loving, tender, yet bold instruction, free from condemnation and the threat of death (eternal separation) (Romans 6:23). This is really a message about love, and it's for everyone in the Body of Christ and unbelievers alike, that wants to be free from the spirit of Jezebel. Some of you might be saying, "You know, I'm not really dealing with this issue of immorality." Then the Lord wants you to be equipped to minister deliverance and counsel from the biblical perspective, and to warn them in love from the true biblical perspective. It's not enough just to say, "I know immorality is no good." We need to be able to break it down with the Bible in love when we're ministering to other people. So this message is for everyone. The whole Sermon on the Mount is for everyone.

Matthew 5:27-30. *"'You have heard that it was said to those of old, 'You shall not commit adultery'" (Mt. 5:27).*

Jesus is saying to His disciples, you have heard the Pharisees teach the Ten Commandments. And the seventh commandment is this: "You shall not commit adultery" (Ex. 20:14). He says, "You've heard their teaching; but they haven't given you the whole message. They've minimized it; they've reduced it to a bare minimum because they don't understand God's heart or His original intention."

So in verse 28 He says, "I'm going to tell you the bigger message that was intended in the heart of God back in Exodus 20, when the Ten Commandments were originally given" (Mt. 5:28, paraphrased). "But I say to you that whoever looks at a woman to lust for her has already committed adultery with her in his heart" (ibid, NKJV). Now this is a revolutionary idea. He's saying, "The Pharisees say that as long as you avoid the physical act of adultery you're free of immorality." Jesus says, "No, you're not. Jesus says, I'm not trying to be mean; I'm trying to be helpful. I want to liberate you. I want you to be exhilarated in your spirit. You have to know that even in looking on a woman to lust, immorality is working in you long before you commit the physical act of adultery." He says, "The problem is there and I want to help you diagnose it so that you can get delivered of it so that you can enter into the freedom and the glory of what I've called you to be as my people."

A Covenant with the Eyes

He goes on to say something even more revolutionary than what He just said in verse 28. Verse 29 is so radical. "If your right eye causes you to sin, pluck it out and cast it from you; for it is more profitable for you that one of your members perish, than for your whole body to be cast into hell" (Mt. 5:29). If your right eye causes you to sin related to immorality, pluck it out. "What?" He says, "Cut your eye out." Now Jesus isn't talking about physical mutilation; He's talking about spiritual self-denial. He's saying, "Be radical in your life choices even though you have to deny yourself in doing so." He says, "What is more profitable, for one of your members to perish or your whole body, your whole person to be thrown into hell?"

In verse 30, He says it a little differently. He says, *"And if your right hand causes you to sin, cut it off and cast it from you; for it is more profitable for you that one of your members perish, than for your whole body to be cast into hell"* (Mt. 5:30). He says, "I'm arguing for your benefit. I want you to see the benefit of embracing this reality in the spirit that I'm presenting to you." In context, Jesus is calling His disciples to the importance of resisting the spirit of immorality, not waiting until physical adultery is presented as a temptation, because long before that it's already pervasive and working in people's lives. Now the Pharisees taught that you didn't have any problems with the spirit of immorality as long as you avoided the physical act. They were unaware that they had a sickness that they were not addressing. That sickness was growing in them, and it was injuring and defiling them but they didn't know it.

So again, Jesus is talking about love right now. He's not talking about strict, religious, rigid standards. He's talking about love and liberty in the Spirit and how to walk in it. Remember the context: just a few verses earlier, in verses 3-12, He gave the eight beatitudes. He said, *"Blessed are the pure in heart"* (Mt. 5:8). He said, "You can have a vibrant spirit. You can be exhilarated in God." He just laid it all out there, talking about how we can be exhilarated in our walk with God. He said, "This will actually minimize your ability to experience God. I'm trying to help you." So this isn't harsh, angry, holiness preaching; He isn't approaching it that way at all.

This Is Not a Comprehensive Teaching on Freedom from Immorality

It's important that we know He isn't giving a comprehensive teaching on freedom from sexual addiction. There are other principles involved in the comprehensive teaching. Later in this chapter I list about seven or eight of them. That's not the point right now. Jesus is identifying two very significant principles in the pursuit of overcoming the spirit of immorality. He's identifying two of them and saying, "Alert, alert, alert! You won't see these two easily. You'll need the revelation of the Spirit to grasp what I'm saying. You don't see what I'm saying." These are revolutionary ideas. That's why He isolates these two. Again, He could have easily added ten or twelve more points that are important in our quest to walk in total victory over immorality. But He gives particular prominence to these two, and many times we don't even think of these two in our desire to walk in liberty.

When You Look To Lust, It's Already Working in You

Here's the first one. Verse 28. He says, "When you look to lust, it's already working in you" (Mt. 5:28, paraphrased). In other words, "Immorality is already powerfully working in you now. Long before the physical act, it's already pervasive and dangerous. Deal with it now. You have a disease you haven't diagnosed, and I'm tipping you off because I love you." They're thinking, "Oh, that's interesting." He says, "You're already entrenched in it. It's already defiling you, but you're not addressing it because you don't think you have a problem." He says, "I'm shining the light on the pervasive problem already working in you. It's damaging you. It's defiling you. It's hurting you now." This is one of the keys to addressing having a vibrant spirit in God. The good news is, this is a treatable sickness, but you have to know it and you have to treat it immediately. It's doable. But not only that: not only is it working in you now, not only is it pervasive and treatable, but the eye gate is the key. Because the Pharisees are putting all their attention on avoiding the physical act of adultery. He says, "The eye gate is the key. Its' how the spirit of immorality grows in you, but not only that: it's the place where you begin to overcome it. You overcome immorality by addressing the eye gate." Technically, that's not really the place where we begin. We begin back in the Beatitudes: the pure in heart see God by encountering God and having a vibrant spirit.

You Have To Make Radical Choices to Deny Your Carnal Appetites

The second main point He's making is in verses 29-30. He says, "Now that you know you have a problem and that the eye gate is the key, you have to deal with it in a radical way. You can't be passive about it. It won't go away on its own. You won't just wake up one day and find that that aggressive spiritual cancer has just disappeared. It doesn't happen that way. You have to be radical. You have to make radical choices that will involve things that are precious to you—plucking out the right eye, cutting off the right hand." And again, He doesn't mean physical mutilation of your body. He means, "No matter how dear it is to you, make the radical choice now, because it won't go away on its own."

Jesus Understands Better Than Anyone Else what Motivates freedom from Immorality

Then He links getting free from immorality to eternal judgment. Now days no one does that. I mean, that's so old-fashioned today in our culture, to link being motivated to obey to eternal judgment. That went out of style some years ago, but it didn't with Jesus. Now He doesn't only link it to eternal judgment, but neither is He shy about it. He's bold about it. Actually, Jesus preached more on hell than anyone else. Jesus understood hell more than anyone else because He created it Himself. He's linking the motivation to walk free from immorality with our eternal destiny in a negative sense. Now again, already in the Beatitudes He gave us the big picture: first the positive, that we could be blessed and have a vibrant spirit, or we could see God. "Blessed are those who see God" (Mt. 5:8, paraphrased). To see God means to experience Him, to feel His presence. He's already given us that primary motivation. So in other words, Jesus is teaching how immorality grows through the eye gate, how it's overcome through the eye gate, and also how dangerous it is if it's left to itself.

Now the issue of walking free from immorality is not a preference issue. Some ministries say, "Well, we don't really address the negative stuff. We like to keep it positive; we like to keep it focused on the love of God." But I say to you, this is a "love of God" issue. This is about loyal love to Jesus. This is about having the capacity in our spirit to experience Jesus in a greater way. This is about loyal love to people whom we might be touching. The whole subject is the subject of love. It's not just that eternal hell is the only motivation, but it is part of the motivation that He gives. I should also say that the spirit of Jezebel has many different expressions than just immorality. But immorality is like an aggressive spiritual cancer, meaning it won't go away by itself. It will grow if left to itself. That's what Jesus is pointing out, because the Pharisees didn't even think they had a problem with it, and it was pervasive in their lives. It was hurting them and they didn't even know it. I mean, it's horrible to have a disease and to not know you have it, and it's treatable if you only knew it.

What Is Sexual Immorality?

This is the big debate in our generation, "What is immorality?" Immorality includes all sexual activity outside the covenant of traditional marriage between one man and one woman. It took about twenty Bible verses put together to come up with that definition. But based on scripture, Immorality includes all sexual activity, whether physical—touching someone in a sexual way; verbal—talking sexually in an inappropriate way; or even in the realm of technology, which is so common today. It's sexual activity in these ways outside of a covenant of marriage between one man and one woman. We will talk in a later chapter about what constitutes a biblical marriage.

Often young people ask, and I understand it, "How far can we go?" You shouldn't go anywhere sexually until you're married. Zero. "In this generation we might say, Oh, really? Why? That sounds a little rigid, a little strict." No, because of love, because Jesus wants us to experience Him, to walk in loyal love to Him and to love our partner in the highest way we can. Young couples tell me, "Well, we're going to be married anyway." I say, "Why would you take the last few months before you make that covenant and live defiled? Why not go to your marriage day with a bright spirit? Why go to your marriage day with this behind you for the last few months?" I mean, if you're involved in that, repent of it and decide that you're going to obey the Lord's leadership, and then on the wedding day have a bright spirit when you make that covenant together.

Don't Give Satan the Legal Right to Oppress and Damage Your Life

Why is Jesus so adamant about this point of immorality? Not because He has some rigid religious standard of strictness; but because He's zealous for love. Because He loves so well and He understands love so well. He knows this: that if we're involved in immorality, we're giving Satan the legal right to oppress and damage our life and relationship. It's like Satan is at the door of the house, pounding at the door, trying to get in. But he can't make entry in a number of ways unless we unlock the door and invite him in. Jesus is saying, "If you walk in immorality, though you can get a bunch of people to back you up and say it's OK, you're giving the key to the one who will torment you. Why do that even a little? Keep him out! He will oppress and damage your heart. He will injure your ability to experience God." So there's no angry tone in this. There's no railing against sin. There's no condemnation, but there is a tender beckoning to enter into the highest and the fullness of what God has. Again, already in the eight Beatitudes He has shown us how to live blessed or exhilarated in our spirit before God.

Make a Lifelong Commitment to the Heart of Your Beloved

The Lord sets all sexual expression within the covenant of marriage. It's a very important point. He puts sexual expression in the covenant of marriage for a very important point. He knows this. He knows this in a way we don't know it. We sort of know it, but He really knows it. He knows that the only place that sexual activity will enrich your life is in the context of a lifelong covenant.

Let me just talk to the guys; it goes both ways, but first I'll address the guys, since mostly the guys should be the initiator of relationships. But ladies, know that all these principles go the other way, too. But let's hypothetically state that a guy is in love with this girl and really likes her; she's so cute, and he says, "You know, I just love her and I want to go forward in sexual ways." The Scriptures say, "No, not until you've made a lifelong covenant to her life story." I mean, you'll engage with her story in the past, the good and the bad, and her story in the future: her pains, her weaknesses, her strengths, her victories, her joys. The things about her life in the decades to come that are exciting, the things that are boring; the things you understand, the things you don't understand. He says, "Only in a context of that kind of commitment will sexual activity enrich you." You need that covenant for longevity, where you willingly participate in her story in all of its facets, both good and bad— in her family, her dreams, her fears—I mean, you get the whole package! In that context, sexual activity will enrich you; but outside of that context, it will injure you and it will injure her in ways you can't even perceive. Now a lot of guys say, "Man, I really love her. But I'm not interested in a fifty-year commitment to hearing her story and figuring all that out. It just sounds hard. She's cute and I think we could have a fun summer together." The Lord says, "Don't dare. It will defile your spirit and hers. It will dull and injure your heart though you don't even know it." It will injure hers.

You Can't Touch Lust without It Increasing In You

You can't touch lust without it increasing in you unless you repent of it; then it can decrease. It's interesting that when David committed adultery, the prophet Nathan came to him in 2 Samuel 12 and said, "David, yes you committed adultery. You sinned against your family. You sinned against her and her family, but what you don't know is that the Lord says you despised the Lord in throwing off His leadership in that adultery" (2 Sam. 12:10). A lot of folks don't think about the fact that they're despising the Lord in sinning against the person that they love but with whom they haven't made a lifelong covenant.

The Perversion Industry Is Reaching New Heights of Immorality

Let's look at these two principles again. Now again, these are a red alert! They're not the whole story of how to get victory, but Jesus says you need revelation from the Spirit on these two because you won't naturally understand them yourself. The number one principle is that the spirit of immorality is already working in you if you look in lust. It's a pervasive problem already damaging you now. So red alert, red alert, emergency! Let's take this at emergency level and not be casual about it. He explained that the gate of the eye is the place where immorality grows and is fueled. On the bright side, the eye gate is one of the places where immorality is cut off and diminished if we make a covenant with our eyes. Now He's talking about looking at a person in person and lusting after them. That's how they would have understood it then, in that day, but in today's day with technology and media what's far more troublesome is what's happening in the media. We know that one of the adversary's main strategies is to use the media to fill the earth with perversion. Imagine how much immorality has increased in the last ten to twenty years. Where will it be in another twenty years? I can't imagine how much the "perversion industry" will be financing much of the technology in new and innovative ways. The new increases in technology aren't all coming from the perversion industry, but many of them are. Where will holograms be in the realm of sexual perversion in twenty and thirty years? I can't even fathom whatever other things they come up with. My point is, it's not just a pervasive problem inside of people. Our culture is going to be completely inundated. This isn't a subject to wait a few years to get serious about.

Three Stages in the Progression of Adultery

Jesus taught here in verse 28 that adultery moves in three stages. It begins with eye adultery; then it grows to heart adultery, or the imagination—sexual fantasies. Then it moves on to physical adultery. The Pharisees didn't appreciate this, because they thought they could obey the seventh of the Ten Commandments, "Thou shalt not commit adultery" (Ex. 20:14, KJV), by just physically avoiding women. Then they would have no sickness to address. Jesus said, "Wrong! You have a problem now, and I love you so much that I'm pointing it out." In the next chapter we will progress in our process of overcoming the spirit of Jezebel, and specifically the spirit of immorality in our generation, by dealing with adultery, fornication and homosexuality at the eye level.

CHAPTER 8

A COVENANT WITH MY EYES AND BODY
The Eye and Hand Symbols

Job 31:1-4 "I have made a covenant with my eyes; how then could I gaze at a virgin? 2 What would be my portion from God above and my heritage from the Almighty on high? 3 Is not calamity for the unrighteous, and disaster for the workers of iniquity? 4 Does not he see my ways and number all my steps?

It's a lot easier to correct sin at the eye gate than it is to put out the raging fires of growing immoral passions. Now Job 31 says it so clearly. Job says, "I have made a covenant with my eyes" (Job 31:1). He said, "I will not look on anything that stirs up lust in my heart" (Job 31:1b, paraphrased). This is a covenant that will greatly enrich our spiritual life. Bob Sorge, in his book, *A Covenant with my Eyes,* says this about the sexual images that we are being bombarded with on a daily basis in our generation;

We're in a war! Sexual Images accost us at every turn-enticing, luring, tempting, seducing. You don't have to be a rocket scientist to see it; it's everywhere. We're hit when we go to school, when we go to work, when we use the computer, when we watch TV, when we go to the grocery store, and even when we drive down the road. Can the barrage be escaped? Like never before, compromise is accessible, affordable, and anonymous. One click on the device in your hand can deliver it to you immediately. Sometimes it seems as though an entire generation is being swept up in a tsunami of sin that is disqualifying them from their divine destiny. Without question, hell has launched an offensive against today's generation to take down their purity and incarcerate them in lifestyles of immorality. (1)

1. A Covenant with My Eyes, Bob Sorge, Oasis House publishing

This is what Jesus is saying in Matthew 5:28. He says, "You have a pervasive problem that's already working in you long before you touch anyone—but you can correct it! It's treatable if you put a focus and attention on the eye gate. It's a spiritual cancer. Don't ignore the eye gate and expect this cancer to go away on its own, this spiritual cancer." David affirmed the same truth in Psalm 101:2-3. He said, "I will walk within my house with a perfect heart, and I will set nothing wicked before my eyes" (Ps. 101:2-3). Now this is a big statement. He says, "I will walk within my house." Our house is the place where we have most familiarity and most privacy. And because our guard is down, our house is typically where we're the most selfish, the most carnal, the laziest, the most unguarded. That's where we can say the most degrading things and our anger can express itself. Again, out in public everything is respectful, and we're going strong, and we're obedient, godly men and women. But David said, "In my house where no one can see me, where I'm most unguarded and most familiar, I will set nothing wicked before my eyes—nothing. Lord, I commit to you. "This is a commitment he's making to God."

If Your Eye Causes You to Sin, Pluck It Out and Cast It from You"

Jesus is talking about how to deal with lust. He says, "Now that you've decided how important the eye gate is, you know you have a problem that's already growing and working within you." The eye gate isn't the whole issue, but it is key. He says, "Now let's take it up a notch. Principle number two is, you have to make radical decisions to alter situations in your life in order to remove things that are inflaming lust in you." He ties it together and He says, "And you make these radical decisions knowing that lust won't go away by itself. But you make them in the knowledge that there's certain judgment coming for people who cast off God's way in this realm of morality."

Now this is a pretty intense approach. In Matt 5:29 Jesus says, *"If your right eye causes you to sin, pluck it out and cast it from you."* That's better than going to hell. Verse 30: *"If your right hand causes you to sin, cast it off. Cut it off and cast if from you."* It's better than going to hell. Again, it's not popular to tie motivation to obedience to going to hell, because "that's just not how people are motivated!" Jesus says, "You're wrong. That's part of the motivation. It's not the whole motivation, but I know how the human heart works and it's true. They'll go to hell. It's real. It's not a tactic. That's really where they'll go if they disregard Me in this area." "Lord, that's pretty intense." Now the eye and the hand are symbols of that which is most precious and most useful in a person's life. Let's take the eye for a moment. The eye speaks of that which is dearest and most precious to your life. I mean, if someone had the option to lose one of the faculties of their body, their eye would be one of the last ones they would lose. It's very, very dear, very cherished, and that's the point. In the ancient world, like today in many places as well, the hand was the symbol of the workforce. The hand was where people made their money.

So the hand relates to that to which increases economics. He says, "I want you to understand that if it comes to removing something precious—I'm not talking about your physical eye but something as precious as your eye." There aren't many other things that are that precious. He says, "If it comes to that, then move it. It could be cable or satellite T.V., or cutting off the internet, or even the mobile phone, to preserve your purity. Move that person out of your life. Get out of that adulterous situation." You might say, I work at a place and they're really into that stuff..."He says, "Cut your right hand off, even if you lose economic advantage." Lose it. Because you have to understand that your eternal destiny is far more important than that precious relationship or that well-paying job or watching that television show, or browsing the internet, or anything else that's near and dear to you. The man says, "But I love her. She means everything to me." I say, "Does she mean your eternal destiny to you?" Some might say, what about grace?" We just cast off God's leadership and claim grace later. You know, that's a dangerous, non-biblical approach to sinning. "You can't have His leadership over your life and the adulterous relationship. Break it."

Jesus Taught More on Hell than Anyone Else In the Bible

Many in the Church have a low view of hell, but Jesus does not. Again, He created it. He taught more on hell than anyone else. I'm talking about unrepentant, immoral people. That's the key. Because you can stumble in immorality, but if you call it sin and declare war on it, the Lord will be with you in your sincerity every step of the way, because you won't get free from the practices in one moment. I mean, that happens occasionally, but ordinarily the freedom comes over time. You can enjoy the Lord even while you're walking on the way to freedom—even though you're stumbling, because you're declaring war on it and calling it sin. In other words, you have an honest, sincere heart, and the Lord says, "I can enjoy My relationship with you and I can help you in that context."

People Go To Hell Because They Refuse the Leadership of Jesus

The point is, don't approach this and say, "Oh no, this is either all or nothing!" No, repent of it and continue to work through it, even though you're struggling, but you're warring against it each step of the way. A lot of people who are in the church world are very lackadaisical about immorality. They say, "No, I'm not going to repent of it. That other church says it's OK!" That view is disastrous. People really will go to hell for denying Jesus' leadership in this area of their life. They don't go to hell because of immorality. They go to hell because they refuse Jesus' leadership. Because we believe that people will go to hell for refusing Jesus' leadership in this area, we speak out boldly—tenderly but boldly; not with a harsh tone, because we love.

We're fighting for love. This is a message about love. The best analogy that will help us understand this message of bold love is that of the doctor, when a lady visits his office and gets a checkup, and she has an aggressive cancer. It's growing fast, but it's treatable if she takes instant, immediate measures. It's aggressive. We're talking about making radical decisions. The doctor says, "You can treat it. But you have to act now, and you have to act radically." But what if the diagnosis is cancer and it's growing fast, but he says, "I know her. I want to stay positive. We're friends. I want to affirm her." So he comes back and gives her the report. She says, "How am I?" "Well, you're OK. I want to keep this positive and upbeat. I want you to feel affirmed. I want you to invite me to the barbeque next week. Everything is fine." The lady dies of cancer. Is that love? Of course that doctor would be charged with malpractice, but beloved, by that same distorted, non-biblical, perverse definition of love, we're operating in malpractice as ministers and citizens of the kingdom of God. We can't redefine love on our terms and affirm immorality because we value the person.

The True Essence of Tolerance

There's really manipulative rhetoric out in the culture today. It's called tolerance. People use that word to mean several different things. There's a very manipulative way that the word tolerance is used. The word tolerance means we value the individual and we see their dignity. That's awesome, and the true essence of what it means to be tolerant. So we tolerate the fact that they have different views because we value them. That's excellent. But that's not the same thing as agreeing with their destructive behavior. See, they have different views, but we value them and we celebrate their humanity, but we love them so much we're going to address the destructive behavior when it's appropriate to address it. So we don't have to choose between valuing them and being straightforward. We can do both, but in the right time in a tone of love.

Sexually Immoral People Will Not Inherit the Kingdom Of God

Look at what the Bible says in 1 Corinthians 6. It's very clear about judgment. It says, *"Do not be deceived. Neither fornicators, nor idolaters, nor adulterers, nor homosexuals, nor sodomites, nor thieves, nor covetous, nor drunkards, nor revilers, nor extortioners will inherit the kingdom of God"* (1 Cor. 6:9-10)—not if they don't repent. If they repent, they fully receive the kingdom for free. If they don't repent, they will not enter into the kingdom of heaven. Now people say, "Yeah, so I get the sodomites and the homosexuals and adulterers, but what is this fornicator thing? Who are they?" Those are the single Christians. There's no covenant of marriage they're violating, but they're involving their lives in immorality, sexual immorality and they're not repenting of it. "Well, we're single, we're not married; we're claiming grace." He says, "I want you to know this. That group of people, if they don't repent, no matter how much they hang out in the church world, are not in the kingdom." That's not a very popular message, but he warned them, "Don't be deceived about this. There's a lot of popular sentiment out there, but they're lying to you; they're not giving you the truth."

Ephesians 5 says the same thing. He's writing this to the Ephesians. He says, "When I was with you, I made this crystal clear. No fornicator has any inheritance in the kingdom" (Eph. 5:5, paraphrased). No! Not one of them. Again, the fornicators are the single people who aren't violating any marriage covenant. In adultery, at least one of the people is married and the covenant is being violated. He says, "Don't let anyone deceive you with their empty words. They're just empty words. It's not the faithful, true witness of the Bible, of God's heart." He says, "The wrath of God comes on these people" (v. 6, paraphrased). He says, "If you love them, be straightforward."

"Well," says the young man, "no one in the church I grew up with addressed this." Well, you've been in deception. The key to being in deception for years is not to stay in it; it's to get out of it. "Well, where I came from, it doesn't make any difference." What we care about is God who loves us so much that He's fighting for our ability to walk in love towards Him, to walk, to receive love from Him and walk in love toward the person we're touching.

The Flame of Desire Will Become an Inferno If Left Unchecked

The danger of lust is that it grows. It's a big danger. It's unbiased. Lust doesn't care who you are. The most dignified person, the most intelligent, triple PhD at Harvard, head of the space department, world banking system, the most powerful personality with the strongest mind, lusts will hold them captive with no bias. It doesn't matter what position or what kind of personality they have, lust has a power of its own that's bigger than they are. Immorality is so dangerous because it grows. It becomes uncontrollable. Now younger people don't think that's true. They're so young, they haven't yet experienced how uncontrollable it is; they may have seen it here and there, but they think to themselves, "I'll dabble with immorality in my twenties. Boys will be boys. I'll sow my wild oats." We make light of it. "Then when I'm in my thirties, I'll control it." It doesn't work that way. "I'll take a little injection of a really aggressive type of cancer, and then in a few years we'll get rid of the cancer!" No, that doesn't make any physical sense. But it's the same logic.

Here's what they don't know. Lust is more powerful and more dangerous and it grows faster than they know. They have no idea what they're touching. They're just having a good time. You know, they're in their college years; they're in their twenties. They haven't yet put together the power of the combination of four things that happens when lust grows unchecked. Let me tell you these four things.

Four Things that happen when Lust grows unchecked by Repentance

Number one: *their heart gets colder*. So they're in their twenties; now they're in their thirties, but their heart is colder than it was in their twenties. **Number two:** *Their mind is darker.* They have more perversion in their memory. They weren't counting on that. They just thought the perversion would go away. It doesn't. It's actually got a bigger stronghold. **Number three:** *Their conscious is hardened;* it's defiled; it's not as responsive as in their twenties. **Number four:** *They have more demonic activity in their life.*

The man says, "Man, I thought I would just play around in my twenties, and then in my thirties I would get serious, have a family, and be a man of God. But it's harder! My heart isn't moving. I thought it would just move on its own." Their heart is colder, their mind is more perverse, their conscious is more defiled, and they have more demonic activity. Then when they're in their forties it's worse than in their thirties. Then in their fifties it's worse than their forties. It keeps getting worse. You need to repent and make radical decisions: cut off the eye and then the hand. I mean, remove the most cherished and even the most costly financially situations, no matter what the cost. Be radical, and be sure of this, if you don't come under His leadership, no matter what they told you in your Sunday school class, you'll end up in the lake of fire. You really will.

Someone says, "Well, I thought if I prayed the sinner's prayer, I would be OK." No. They told you a lie. This is real. The man says, "Wow. This is pretty intense! I'm in my thirties, and my heart isn't moving towards God like I thought it would." Well, you're in lot worse condition on the inside. Your forties will be worse. You know, we invite demons into our life by our activities. They can't get in unless we open the door. This sounds cute, but demons are expensive. I mean, you have to pay money to do some of these things to get those demons. Then you have to feed your pet demon for years because you have costly habits now. Then you get tired of it and it costs a lot of money to get rid of those demons. I mean, the whole thing is expensive. It costs you a lot of money, a lot of time, and a lot of relationships. Demons are destructive. A lot of people in this generation will pick up a lot of demons in their twenties, casually claiming the grace of God in a false way.

Flee Immorality Like Your Life Is In the Balance

This is a very important passage. Paul urges us to flee sexual immorality (1 Cor. 6:18). Flee immorality like your life is in the balance. Imagine that you're in a park and you look across the way and a wild lion escaped from the zoo. There it is chasing you. Paul says to flee it like a lion is coming after you, because in 1 Peter 5:8, the devil is compared to a devouring lion. That lion is aggressive. But you're thinking, "Well, I think I'll just chill out and finish my lunch. Maybe when he comes I'll invite him to participate." He will have you for lunch! He's wild. He has no reasoning and no mercy. He will destroy you. You had better flee. People don't flee immorality. They kind of avoid it occasionally. He says, "Don't avoid it; run for your life from immorality."

Then he gives the reason, and it's an unusual reason. Or it's a reason that surprises us at first. He says, "Let me tell you why you had better run for your life." It goes beyond just avoiding that one party: I mean, turn off the Internet, don't speak to women in sexual ways, don't touch them, and don't go see the movies. Flee this thing like you're running for your life, because this lion is truly chasing you. It's not a game. He says, "Let me tell you why. Every sin that a man does is outside of his body" (1 Cor. 6:18b, paraphrased). When he steals money, that's outside of his body. But a man who commits adultery sins against his own body. That's an unusual concept. "What do you mean he sins against his body?" That's the only sin whereby we sin against our body. Or it's the only one that Paul identifies, is probably a more accurate way to say it.

God Will Give Them Up To Uncleanness in the Lusts of their Hearts

In Romans 1 Paul elaborates: he develops what he means by sinning against your own body by immorality. Now look at verses 24-28: this is a very sobering, even kind of terrifying passage.

Verse 24. "God . . . gave them up to uncleanness" (Rom. 1:24). Now you'll notice three times it says God gave them up. He's giving them up in a greater measure, in a greater way. He's giving them up to greater perversion. Now first He gives them up and says, "Are you going to repent?" They say, "No." Then He gives them up in a greater sphere of perversion. "Are you repenting?" "No."

Then He gives them up to a final sphere of perversion. And so follow this. It's talking about immorality here. He says God gave them up to their uncleanness. They wouldn't repent of it Again, in our church world we have Bible verses to back up the grace of God where it's OK to do it. God will give a person up to their uncleanness in the lust of their hearts and they'll continue to dishonor their body. That's a terrifying concept. This passage explicitly lays out the process. If they repent they'll be totally forgiven, and they begin to experience deliverance. Fantastic! If they don't, we're talking about the negative here. This works for guys or gals, old or young. He says, "God gave them up to vile passions. For even their women exchanged the natural use for what is against nature. Likewise also the men" (Rom. 1:26-27). It's talking about homosexuality. He says, "Likewise also the men leaving the natural use of the woman, burned in their lust for one another, men with men committing what is shameful, and receiving in themselves the penalty of their error which was due"(Rom. 1:27).

Here's the point that I want to highlight; Paul is saying they receive in their body, in themselves, in their body and their soul, a penalty that's working. The penalty increases if they don't repent. Oh, this is terrifying! This is what Paul means when he says they sin against their body. He says they open the door for a penalty to begin to operate inside of their body and inside of their soul and their spirit. Then, if they still don't repent, it gets worse and worse. Verse 28: God will give them over to a debased mind; a depraved mind.

God Will Lift the Natural Restraints That Protect Us from Perversion

Now what does it mean for God to give them up, to give them over? It means that He lifts the natural restraints with which He designed the human frame. Every single person, believer and unbeliever, has natural restraints built in us that repel perversion at the beginning. Something in us; says, "I don't think this is right." When we're really young and someone touches us, we say, "No, this doesn't seem right." There's a natural restraint. But we don't have the power to obey that restraint in the full sense, so we cry out to God for salvation. That's part of our journey to the Lord. If we yield ourselves to it, the Lord says, "I will lift the restraint in a greater measure. They'll go from uncleanness to vile passion; if they don't yield and repent, I'll give them a depraved mind." Now God isn't giving them the depraved mind; Really, He's just letting them have what they chose. That's the penalty. It's not that He's doing something to them; He's simply lifting the restraint and saying, "You want lust? You can have more of it, but you'll have it in a measure that you don't understand and you won't like. You want lust and you don't want My leadership? Here, take the lust." So they're released at one level and some people repent. Others say, "Oh, I can't get satisfaction. I have to have more."

He says, "You had better back off of this." Then He releases them and gives them over. He lifts the restraint at a greater measure. Finally, it's a debased mind. I mean, the most terrifying measure. Now there's a very important verse that describes this. 2 Peter 2:19, describing false teachers who teach the Bible. They promise you liberty in the realm of morality. 2 Peter 2:19. They promise liberty in sexual experience. They think they'll be satisfied and find liberty. People say, "I want liberty in my sexuality," but they end up in bondage with cravings they can never satisfy. The cravings get deeper, darker, more perverse, and less satisfying the more they go on. They're looking for liberty and satisfaction. They get bondage and insatiable cravings that never, ever stop. That's what they get. Well, so much for the liberty message, because that's what they want. Our nation is crying out for sexual liberty. They'll walk straight into horrific bondage with cravings that will be deeper and darker and less and less satisfying the further they get from God. Oh, it's terrifying!

When they're finally given over to a debased mind, all the restraints are lifted. They're in total bondage. Literally, they can't go for two minutes without thinking perverse thoughts. They could be the leader of a great financial empire, but even in the midst of their business meetings there are immoral thoughts in their mind. They're depraved. They think its liberty. They have no satisfaction. They're pushing new boundaries and getting more demons.

The Danger of Lust Is That God Judges it even in this Age

The danger of lust is that God judges it even in this age. I've already talked about how He judges it eternally. He judges it now as well, but here's the good news: that's a love message. It's Because of love. He judges us to get us to turn us away from what will ultimately kill us. He says, "I will wake them up. I'm not letting them go in this spiritual cancer without an intervention. I love them so much, I will remove their options and put them against a wall. I will ambush them and see if they'll say yes to me." A lot of times they do and a lot of times they don't. He wants to stop the progression that's working in them, so He judges. Some people say, "Well, the God of the Old Testament judges, and Jesus, the God of the New Testament, does not." That's absolute biblical confusion.

The God of the Old and the New Testament is identically the same God. He loves and judges in both Testaments and He only judges for the sake of love: to remove the things that hinder love. We can see in Revelation 2, concerning His church, that he clearly warns them that he will judge them if they don't wake up and deal with the cancer slowly eating away at their lifeline. I want to urge you to read Revelation 2 carefully, because you need to be equipped in these verses for yourself so that when some well-meaning, distorted believer comes along and tells you it's OK to live in immorality in the name of grace because everything is fine, you'll have a way to stand and say, "No, that's not what the Bible says." They might say, "Our church says it's OK." But we must be equipped to say, "It doesn't matter what your church says." Jesus loves me and I love His leadership. I want you to be able to know these verses. If it's not even personal for you but it's someone to whom you're ministering, they may say, "Well, I heard that it's OK now. No one is preaching on sin anymore!" You say, "Well, Jesus is." And then you can add, "And so am I!" Tell them, "I'm with Jesus," and then give them the verses in Revelation 2. Then there's much more besides. We have to operate in the opposite spirit of immorality, and progressively we get free.

Now we get forgiven instantaneously. We can have a first-class standing before God. I mean, the moment we repent we can stand with confidence, as a first-class citizen. I don't mean that the bondage is done; we're still stumbling, but we're warring against it, so we have integrity and sincerity in our relationship with Him. He smiles at us. He says, "I delight in you. Keep warring and I'm with you. Cry out to Me. Never, ever let go of the battle"; and I tell you there's an integrity and there's a sincerity in your relationship with Him even though you're in weakness. He can and He will help you.

"Receive With Meekness the Implanted Word, Which Is Able To Save"

James 1. said, *"Lay aside all filthiness . . . Receive with meekness the implanted word, which is able to save your souls"* (Js. 1:21). Now he doesn't mean it's able to forgive you right now; it's able to heal your soul.

Now first we have to lay aside all filthiness. Some people hope that they'll go to bed one night and wake up without filthiness. Jesus won't decide this for you. You have to say no to immorality at the eyes, and when it requires the cutting off of the hand and the plucking of the eye, those cherished and even costly financial decisions, you'll make them.

He says, "OK, you've laid aside filthiness. Now your heart is still raw. Your heart is still under the power of the sin, but you've made the choices so that now we're in the right position together." He says, "Receive the word implanted." Now the word implanted is more than a Bible study. It's more than just hearing a Sunday morning sermon, taking some notes and talking about it with a friend afterwards. The word implanted means the word becomes personal. It's a part of your conversation with Jesus and the seed is growing. It takes time for it to grow as an implanted seed. But it's in you. It's not Bible information; it's part of your conversation with God.

Overcoming the spirit of Jezebel

Proverbs 5-7. Young men, old men read this. Some guy told me when I was around twenty years old to read Proverbs 5-7 every day. I said, "OK…" I didn't even know what it was, and I read it, and it's the most descriptive three chapters. The entire passage isn't about adultery, but mostly it describes how costly adultery is. Proverbs tells us, "If you do this, if you go in this direction, you'll lose your money, you'll lose everything you've worked for. You will lose your job, your family, your reputation, your destiny. You'll lose your children. You will lose everything." It says it over and over like a hard-hitting hammer. I urge you read Proverbs 5-7 regularly. In my early days, in my twenties and thirties, I didn't hear these chapters preached on much: Now in my 40's and when I get into my 50's in a few years, I'm committing to read and preach regularly from these chapters, and tell men to go for it. I want to really stir people up to these chapters.

CHAPTER 9

LGBT DISCRIMINATION GAY MARRIAGE - CIVIL RIGHTS CIVIL DISOBEDIENCE OR MORAL DISOBEDIENCE

In our society today there is an increasing move towards an acceptance of a culture of sexual immorality, in the name of tolerance and constitutional rights. Many compare this movement of acceptance of immorality, specifically concerning the tolerance of homosexual and lesbian rights, with the Civil Rights movement and the desegregation of the races, with the outlawing of discrimination and Jim Crow laws. This is troubling to me as a Pastor that grew up in Urban America and have watched the demise of the traditional family and the effect it has had on our communities. I believe countercultural attitudes toward sexual responsibility has played an important role in creating the crisis that confronts African-Americans today. The decline of the African-American family was triggered almost exclusively by a secular-liberal culture which, among other things, actually celebrated the demise of the traditional family.

This increasing movement towards the acceptance of immorality in our society and the philosophy connecting LGBT behavioral rights with the Civil Rights movement is a calculated deception that the LGBT agenda has strategically employed to achieve their goals to normalize this lifestyle. Their strategy is to hook the LGBT movement to the man of Love from the African-American community, Dr. Martin Luther King Jr., and lump their movement of gay marriage equality and sexually immoral behavioral rights into the same discussion with Civil Rights and racial equality.

Knowing that America honors both the life and noble work of the Rev. Martin Luther King Jr., a Bible-believing Christian minister who did more to advance the cause of race-based civil rights than perhaps any other person in recent history, and knowing that the legislative process in America in the latter part of the 20th century and beyond, has been sympathetic to the black plight in discrimination and systemic racism, the LGBT community has attempted to prey on the sensitivities of this process, and on unsuspecting, uninformed African-American leaders, to connect to our movement for racial sameness and equality. They attempt to compare their quest for their immoral behavioral rights to same sex marriage, to our Human rights to racial sameness and the constitutionality of racial equality, by attempting to push a false scientific ideology that Homosexuals and Gays were Born This Way.

If the nation can be convinced they were born this way, they can connect their Born This Way ideology with the African-American movement for racial equality with White people based on the same premise of there being no physiological difference between Black and White that would warrant any preferential treatment of White people, or discrimination of Black people.

One of the dangers in African-Americans embracing this philosophy is that we end up embracing a lifestyle that allows us to accept a behavior modification that further minimizes and eventually eliminates our African-American male-father influence in our communities, further stunting the development of young men in our communities, who are already being targeted and gunned down at an alarming rate in this generation.

The inevitable end of this process will completely remove fathers from our homes and further sociologically hinder our community advancement. Already, at present in our African-American communities over 70% of our children are being raised without fathers in the homes. This has been proven to adversely affect our young men growing up without a male role model in the home.

Regrettably – every year - opportunist "LGBT" activist quickly swoop in, picking the live flesh from MLK's character-based "dream," to advance their own behavior-based nightmare. In what amounts to a sort of soft racism, this mostly white, left-wing faction has, over the years, disingenuously and ignobly hitched its little pink wagon to a civil rights movement that, by contrast, is built upon the genuine and noble precepts of racial equality and humanitarian justice.

What was MLK's Position on the Homosexual Lifestyle?

What was MLK's position on the homosexual lifestyle and so-called "gay rights"? While he said little in public on the issue, what he did say made his viewpoint abundantly clear. Unlike the "LGBT" lobby, I'll let Dr. King speak for himself.

In 1958, while writing an advice column for "Ebony Magazine," Dr. King responded to a young "gay" man looking for guidance. To avoid being accused of "cherry-picking," here is the exchange in its entirety:

Question: *My problem is different from the ones most people have. I am a boy, but I feel about boys the way I ought to feel about girls. I don't want my parents to know about me. What can I do? Is there any place where I can go for help?*

Answer: *Your problem is not at all an uncommon one. However, it does require careful attention. The type of feeling that you have toward boys is probably not an innate tendency, but something that has been culturally acquired. Your reasons for adopting this habit have now been consciously suppressed or unconsciously repressed. Therefore, it is necessary to deal with this problem by getting back to some of the experiences and circumstances that led to the habit. In order to do this I would suggest that you see a good psychiatrist who can assist you in bringing to the forefront of conscience all of those experiences and circumstances that led to the habit. You are already on the right road toward a solution, since you honestly recognize the problem and have a desire to solve it.*

No amount of leftist spin can muddy Dr. King's lucid position on the homosexual lifestyle. He recognized it as a "culturally acquired" "problem" in need of a "solution" – a "habit" stemming from a series of negative "experiences and circumstances."

Although homosexual activists desperately cling to the fact that, after his death, Dr. King's wife, Coretta Scott King, did voice some level of support for the homosexual political agenda, the undeniable reality remains that, based upon his own words, Dr. King supported neither homosexual conduct nor "LGBT" political activism. Indeed, it strains credulity to suggest that MLK would have thrown his weight behind a political movement hell-bent on justifying sexual appetites and behaviors that he properly identified as "a problem" demanding "a solution" – a "type of feeling" that requires "careful attention" – up to and including "seeing a good psychiatrist."

No, MLK was a Christian minister who both embraced and articulated the biblical "love the sinner, hate the sin" model on homosexuality. Every Christian should follow his lead. After all, it is the lead set by Christ Himself.

The Inevitable end of the Present Moral Decline of Sexuality in this Generation

Presently in the second decade of the 21st century it is politically and culturally incorrect for anyone, even ministers of the gospel, to express any objection to so-called alternative lifestyles of Homosexuality and Lesbianism in human sexuality. Anyone that does object to this lifestyle of immorality are labeled intolerant and unenlightened, or worse yet, Ignorant. It seems as if our nation is on sliding scale down to moral oblivion with its moral standards.

For example in 2012 an assistant football coach at Penn State University was indicted and convicted of having sex with over 15 boys, minors, in the university football locker room showers over a 12 year period, and sentenced to 60 years in prison. During this trial and ordeal many in society repudiated and repulsed this coach's behavior, as we should have. The public outrage directed at Penn State and the Head Football Coach Joe Paterno for allowing such behavior on campus was unrelenting and merciless. But I could not help but think how hypocritical a society we are to condemn this act, but yet contribute to its climate with the passing of Gay and Lesbian legislation, in the Gay marriage debate.

My point is this, 30 years ago when I was a 12 year old, in the 6th grade there was a young man in our community that was gay. This behavior, not only was repudiated in the same manner, but most states had laws against sodomy, and homosexuality was medically listed as a psychiatric disease, and the very mention of lesbian and homosexual relations were repudiated and repulsed just like the assistant coach's acts with these boys in the football locker room at Penn State. However, 30 years later the homosexual agenda in our nation has had the laws against sodomy taken off the books of almost every state in the union. It's no longer listed as a psychiatric disease, and it's even being challenged biblically as a behavior that should not be looked at as a sin. It has been embraced, and even pushed off on society as morally tenable and socially acceptable. I can't help but think what our society will look like 30 years from now, if we continue going the direction were going with the sliding scale of moral standards.

This very act in Penn State will also be pushed off on society as a morally tenable and acceptable lifestyle alternative for men to have sex with boys. It's already being lobbied for in the courts in many countries throughout the world by NAMBLA - The North American Man/Boy Love Association - a pedophile and pederasty advocacy organization in the United States. It works to abolish age of consent laws criminalizing adult sexual involvement with minors. Where does it stop? How will we stand in African-America concerning these issues in society today when it is one of the issues affecting the young men in our communities?

Without question, this agenda has launched an offensive against today's African-American young men as well as the generation at large, to confuse the sexuality of this age and to take down the purity of this generation, imprisoning them in lifestyles of destructive immorality, destroying traditional families at such an alarming rate, there's a new strategy to redefine the family structure. They're calling it the "Modern Family." At the root of the modern family is confused and redefined roles for father, mother, girls and boys.

The Agenda behind All Sexual Immorality

The spirit of Jezebel in this age and its atheistic agenda is the spirit behind gender confusion. I believe this spirit – Jezebel - is the spirit behind the LGBT and Gay marriage agenda. This is what's behind the pornographic industry's multi-billion dollar industry. But God has a solution. God has a remedy for those that want to be free and overcome this spirit in this generation.

How Jesus dealt in love with those in His community in Sexual Immorality

Many people, both Christians and non-Christians alike, don't readily associate Jesus ministering to or having anything to say about the sexual sins of Adultery or Homosexuality. Many only attribute standards against those vices to the Old Testament law. And they attempt to associate Jesus' teachings to a more accepting doctrine or philosophy of Grace to the love message, that doesn't mention anything about homosexuality or sexual immorality. However, sexual immorality is addressed by Jesus in His ministry, and it is directly tied to His ministry to the sick. He also shows His method of dealing with sexual immorality through His message to the adulteress in John 8. The following is how Jesus ministered to those in his community entangled in homosexuality. The bible teaches that Jesus went where they were with (WISDOM) teaching, with (CONVICTION) preaching and with (COMPASSION) healing;

Matthew 9:35 Then Jesus went about all the cities and villages, teaching in their synagogues, preaching the gospel of the kingdom, and healing every sickness and every disease among the people.

The Hebrew word for "Disease," coming straight from the Strong's concordance on Hebrew root meanings for biblical words is "Malakia" 3119 (ma-ak-ee'-ah) Meaning 1) SOFTNESS 2) in the NT INFIRMITY, debility, bodily weakness, sickness ORIGIN: from 3120; TDNT - 4:1091,655; n f Usage: AV - disease 3;3

This word is from the root "Malakos" 3120 (mal-ak-os) MEANING: 1) soft, soft to the touch 2) metaph. in a bad sense 2a) EFFEMINATE 2a1) of a CATAMITE 2a2) of a boy kept for HOMOSEXUAL relations with a man 2a3) of a male who submits his body to unnatural lewdness 2a4) of a male prostitute Origin: of uncertain affinity;
 adj USAGE: AV - soft 3, effeminate 1; 4

The word "EFFEMINATE" means having Feminine qualities untypical of a man: not manly in appearance or manner. The word "CATAMITE" means a boy kept by a pederast. "A PEDERAST" is a lover of boys. A pederast is one that practices anal intercourse especially with a boy.

This activity must be abnormal and unnatural because Jesus corrected it. This activity must be a disorder because Jesus cured it. This activity must be harmful because Jesus prayed for the victims to be healed. - Then Jesus went about all the cities and villages, teaching in their synagogues, preaching the gospel of the kingdom, and healing every sickness and every DISEASE among the people. Matt 9:35

The Fight against Homosexuality: Don't fight the attraction fight its right to dictate your actions

I'm convinced that the battle with deliverance from homosexuality and same sex attraction is the same battle with heterosexuality and opposite sex attraction. Don't fight the attraction. Fight its right to dictate your actions. As a man born in a home with a praying father and mother, that kept me from Satan's attempt of any type of sexual abuse, and from any presentation, other than sex being between a man to a woman, my flesh wants any and every pretty woman that it sees. But since the bible says fornication and adultery is immoral and a sin, I have to tell my flesh No! She's off limits, because she's not my wife. The fight against homosexuality is the same. It must begin and end, not with trying to fight the attraction, but with the biblical fact that the bible is the word of God. It is the moral compass for humanity, it is what I want to dictate my actions. And the bible says it's wrong.

For whatever sociological-spiritual reasons, stemming from either sexual abuse, your family upbringing, how u were raised, and-or even, How You Were Born, (we were all born in sin) you have the attraction. But tell yourself, NO! Because the Bible calls it sin. And then war against it with the Word of God. If you find yourself doing what you know is against Biblical sexuality, confess it, repent of it, press delete on your spiritual hard drive and start fresh the next moment, warring against the sin again, in and with the word of God. Keep getting up and telling yourself, self, you are forgiven! Keep on living! Do this, just like any heterosexual that struggles with sexual sins, until your flesh is transformed and totally delivered from its sinful dictates. But don't use the excuse because I was born this way and because I have the attraction this is who I am. YOU CAN BE BORN AGAIN (John 3:2). You can be transformed by the renewing of your mind and be delivered from YOU (Romans 12:2). It all begins by saying, YES to Jesus, and NO to you. Biblically, change is no less an expectation for the homosexual than it is for the porn addict, the liar, the murderer or anyone else who has been under the power of sin. So the question is not "Can a homosexual change?" but "What might change look like for the one who has been trapped in homosexual confusion but has now decided to follow Jesus Christ?"

Briefly stated, substantive change is the fruit of a deepening relationship with God. It is not the result of self-engineered grasping for the ring of holiness but is a natural result of the life-changing revelation of His glory (Jer. 29:11-14; Heb. 11:6) and the transformation of the will that occurs in His presence (Phil. 2:13). The more often we encounter Him and the more deeply, the more transformed we become in our inner man.

Change for those struggling with same-sex attraction occurs on the level of: 1) behavior, 2) belief, 3) identity and 4) desire. It may also involve deliverance from demonic strongholds and family-line curses, the unmasking of hidden roots of idolatry, fear, unbelief, un-forgiveness, the renouncing of ungodly judgments and vows, the healing of emotional wounds, as well as the impartation of missing developmental pieces, such as affirmation and love.

What Science says about Homosexuality and a so-called Gay Gene?

Matt Slick in His research on whether Homosexuals were born gay states 2 interesting reasons why this argument is without merit; (www.carm.org.)

One of the arguments offered by those in support of homosexuality is that homosexuality is an orientation that people are born with, and it has the same moral value as the hair color someone has at birth. The implication is that since they are said to be born gay, then it is normal and morally acceptable. The media seems to support this idea, and it is a common position held to justify the behavior. But there are two problems with this position.

First of all, there are a plethora of studies with conflicting results and conclusions on both sides of the argument. Nevertheless, we could quickly consider studies that deal with identical twins. If genetics determines sexual orientation, then it should be manifested when studying twins who share the exact same genetic information. However, that isn't the case. Consider this . . .

There is no evidence for strong genetic influence on same-sex preference among MZ twins, 6.7 % are concorcant. DZ twin pairs are 7.2% concordant. Full-siblings are 5.5 % concordant. Clearly, the observed concordance rates do not correspond to degrees of genetic similarity. None of the comparisons between MZ twins and others are even remotely significant. If same-sex romantic attraction has a genetic component, it is massively overwhelmed by other factors. As argued above, it is more likely that any genetic influence, if present, can only be expressed in specific and circumscribed social structures." [underline added]

In addition, genetic information that supports heterosexual attraction is more likely to be passed to offspring than would homosexual genetic information since homosexual practice does not produce offspring. It would seem, as the study states, that homosexuality is not genetically based. Therefore, homosexuality is a learned behavior and should be called a preference and not an orientation.

Second, to carry the excuse that homosexuality is genetically based to its logical conclusion, then men born with a natural attraction to young boys should also be considered as having a legit mate sexual orientation with its accompanying moral propriety. Or, are we to say that only homosexual attraction is genetic and morally good where pedophilia is not? If so, why the double standard? And, to step further into the abyss, what do we do with those who are born with the tendency to lie, covet, hate, and steal? Shouldn't they all be morally acceptable as well since that is how we are born? If not, why not?

The problem with using genetics as an excuse to justify behavior is that whatever tendency we might be born with must be considered normal. This includes lying, pedophilia, homosexuality and adultery and rape. But, such a logical inference will not be acceptable to the pro-homosexual community because selective statistics and discriminatory reasoning are offered to justify their behavior.

Another editorial on this issue of "Born This Way" written by freelance writer David Benkof – (www.dailycaller.com 5:57 PM 03/19/2014) - also substantiates the scientific evidence from two gay scholars that say that it is "ludicrous to think the there is a gay gene," in their study on Homosexuality; - (Nobody is 'born that way,' gay historians say) - Sexual orientations cannot be innate

Journalists trumpet every biological study that even hints that gayness and straightness might be hard-wired, but they show little interest in the abundant social-science research showing that sexual orientation cannot be innate. The scholars I interviewed for this essay were variously dismayed or appalled by this trend.

For example, historian Dr. Martin Duberman, founder of the Center for Lesbian and Gay Studies, said "no good scientific work establishes that people are born gay or straight." And cultural anthropologist Dr. Esther Newton (University of Michigan) called one study linking sexual orientation to biological traits ludicrous: "Any anthropologist who has looked cross-culturally (knows) it's impossible that that's true, because sexuality is structured in such different ways in different cultures."
While biology certainly plays a role in sexual behavior, no "gay gene" has been found, and whatever natural-science data exists for inborn sexual orientations is preliminary and disputed. So to date, the totality of the scholarly research on homosexuality indicates gayness is much more socio-cultural than biological.

Chose This Way or Born This Way

Many people attempt to connect the Homosexual agenda to gain a foothold and dovetail its immoral movement onto the Civil Rights movement; by arguing that they were born with this dysfunctional sexuality. And that it's not an immoral choice to express my desires in this way to another man, as a man, or to another woman, as a woman. However, this argument is untenable. Below is an article written for Charisma magazine by Doctor Michael Brown that nails the door shut on this argument scientifically and physiologically.

If there were reputable scientific evidence that some people were born homosexual, I would have no problem accepting this. After all, my theology tells me that as human beings, we are all created in God's image and yet we are a fallen race, and so all of us carry aspects of that fallen nature to the core of our being, and that could theoretically include homosexuality.

But the fact is that there is simply no reputable scientific evidence that anyone is born gay.

As stated by gay activist and history professor John D'Emilio, "'Born gay' is an idea with a large constituency, LGBT and otherwise. It's an idea designed to allay the ingrained fears of a homophobic society and the internalized fears of gays, lesbians and bisexuals. What's most amazing to me about the 'born gay' phenomenon is that the scientific evidence for it is thin as a reed, yet it doesn't matter. It's an idea with such social utility that one doesn't need much evidence in order to make it attractive and credible."

In other words, because the "born gay" idea has proved so useful, the fact that there's virtually no scientific support for the theory hardly matters. It's an idea that has worked wonders for gay activists and their allies.

As noted years ago by gay scientist Simon LeVay, "There [was] a survey in The New York Times that broke down people on the basis of whether they thought gays and lesbians were born that way or whether it was a lifestyle choice. Across the board, those who thought gays and lesbians were born that way were more liberal and gay friendly."

And so, the argument goes, "If I'm born this way, how can my attractions be wrong? And if I'm born this way, how can you expect me to change?"

Of course, even if no one is born gay, that doesn't mean that homosexual attractions are not deeply rooted. In most cases, those feelings are very deeply rooted to the point that many gay men and women truly believe they were born gay.

And even if no one is born gay, that doesn't mean that homosexual attractions are easily changed. In most cases, they are not.

But why base a so-called civil-rights movement on lies? Why not tell the truth?

One of the most gay-friendly professional organizations in our country is the American Psychological Association, and yet even the APA <u>states</u> that, "There is no consensus among scientists about the exact reasons that an individual develops a heterosexual, bisexual, gay, or lesbian orientation."

Similarly, in England, the pro-gay Royal College of Psychiatrists <u>recently backtracked</u> on an earlier statement that homosexuality was biologically determined, now <u>saying</u> that "sexual orientation is determined by a combination of biological and postnatal environmental factors." And while they stated clearly their belief that homosexuality was not a mental disorder and that it should be accepted, they added, "It is not the case that sexual orientation is immutable or might not vary to some extent in a person's life."

That's why psychiatrist Nathaniel S. Lehrman, former chairperson of the Task Force on Religion and Mental Health said in 2005, "Researchers now openly admit that after searching for more than 20 years, they are still unable to find the 'gay gene'" (in the Journal of American Physicians and Surgeons).

Why then do we constantly hear about people being born gay? First, it has worked wonders for gay activism; second, many gays and lesbians believe it to be true, since as far back as they can remember, they felt that they were different.

But political expediency and personal feelings do not change the facts, and those facts remain the same: There is no clear scientific evidence that anyone is born gay

According to lesbian researcher <u>Lisa Diamond</u>, "The queer community has been obsessed with cultivating the idea that we all have fixed sexual identities. We've crafted terrific narratives and political platforms based on the notions that all gays are 'born that way.' But what if sexuality is more complex? What if biology actually intersects with environment, time, culture and context? Could we possibly be more fluid than we've supposed?"

Camille Paglia, a social critic, academic, feminist and lesbian, was even more blunt, famously stating in her book Vamps and Tramps, "Our sexual bodies were designed for reproduction. ... No one is born gay. The idea is ridiculous ... homosexuality is an adaptation, not an inborn trait."

Paglia also asked, "Is the gay identity so fragile that it cannot bear the thought that some people may not wish to be gay? Sexuality is highly fluid, and reversals are theoretically possible."

Remarkably, when a school chaplain in Tasmania, Australia, posted Paglia's opinion on social media, there was an outcry against him, causing him to issue a public apology: "I've made a mistake and learnt from it. I'm deeply sorry for any offence I've caused. I was very careless in posting that image for discussion. I will work with my employers to ensure there is no repeat."

Despite this apology, he was still fired—and the organization he worked for was Christian! That is how toxic today's climate has become, and yet this chaplain simply posted the accurate reflections of a lesbian academic. How could this be considered hateful or bigoted?

Again, this does not mean that same-sex attractions and desires are not deeply rooted in some people's lives, nor does it mean that they chose to be gay. (You can choose to act on your attractions but that doesn't mean you chose to have the attractions.)

It simply means that one of the major gay-activist talking points, one that has even infiltrated parts of the church, is based on lies, not truth.

It's time we speak the truth in love. Lies never help anyone in the long run.

Michael Brown is author of Can You Be Gay and Christian? Responding With Love and Truth to Questions About Homosexuality and host of the nationally syndicated talk radio show The Line of Fire on the Salem Radio Network. He is also president of FIRE School of Ministry and director of the Coalition of Conscience. Follow him at AskDrBrown on Facebook or at @drmichaellbrown on Twitter.

Regardless of what the Transvestite community might try to say concerning men that feel as if they were meant to be women, and women that feel that they were meant to be men, this is a physiological impossibility. The standard and guidelines for the birthing and purpose of men and women are outlined in God's manual for life, the Bible, for the functioning and operation of His prize creation – Human Beings. God's standard of male and female relationships and marriage is given in Genesis 1:27

So God created man in his own image, in the image of God created he him; male and female created he them.28 And God blessed them, and God said unto them, Be fruitful, and multiply, and replenish the earth, and subdue it:

The Woman - A Womb – Man, the Receiver of Seed

A man cannot reproduce with another man; neither can a woman reproduce with another woman. Genesis 2:23 says she shall be called woman because she was taken out of man. The word woman is a combination of two words, the word "womb" and the word "Man." A woman is actually a man with a womb. The womb is where the man with the womb – womb-man, carries the fetus. The word female is a combination of the words "fetus" and "male." So a female is actually a male with the ability to carry a fetus. If the woman was born with a womb she was born to be a Womb-Man, a carrier and reproducer of life. If the man was born with a penis he was born to be a Man, the giver and reproducer of life.

The Man – The Giver of Seed

The man gives the woman seed; the woman receives that seed, reproduces that seed and gives the man children. It takes opposites to produce life. The man was meant to be a giver. A woman was made to be a receiver. The woman's body was made to receive-in seed. The man's body was made to give-out seed. Nothing on his body was created to receive in, only give out. Even the opening that another demented man might try to force his instrument of giving into, was an opening created to give out, not receive in. It was for the giving out of refuse, waste from the body.

The opening on the woman's body was designed especially for the man's giving instrument to receive in that she might take in the seed that the man gives and reproduce children. Even though men and women have misappropriated their functions and purposes for one another, the creator God, the manufacturer has never changed his mind or his purpose for mankind. Many that are proponents of homosexuality and lesbianism purport that they were born that way. However, this is a physiological impossibility. You were born with the equipment you were born with to fulfill the purpose for that which you were given was created for. A construction worker is given a hammer to hammer nails. He's not given a hammer to screw in nails. If a man was born with a penis, he was born to give seed into a womb to reproduce life. If a woman was born with a womb, she was born to receive seed into her womb to reproduce life. But for those that continue to insist that they were born the way they behave, I don't advocate arguing this fact of life that I just detailed in this section. All I say to you is; Jesus said in St. John 3:3-6, YOU CAN BE BORN AGAIN.

Prides expression in an Immoral Generation

This immoral way of choosing to believe and live is the expression of man's pride resisting the leadership and rule of God for their own rule in the earth. As a result of this pride they have sought knowledge of who they are and what they were created for, everywhere except the manufacturer - God. If the computer system that I am producing this material on breaks down I wouldn't look to a manual on how to repair a refrigerator. No! I would look to the manual of the manufacturer who built this system. Well, God being the manufacturer of mankind left a manual – The Holy Bible, The Torah, The Pentateuch – to have and to use not only to fix the system when it breaks down but for us to know how to operate the system so that it functions correctly. We must stand on God's word and know what he says about our life and the issues of life. Just because we struggle with issues of sin and immorality in our lives is not cause to rewrite the manual. We must stick with what God says, regardless of the issues we struggle with in life.

CHAPTER 10

A DREAM OF THE COMING EXPRESSION OF JEZEBEL IN THE PUBLIC SQUARE

One night some months ago I had a dream that I was being made uncomfortable by public homosexual acts in my presence, happening right next to me at a bus stop. (I should state here that I would also be uncomfortable by public heterosexual acts happening in my presence at a bus stop) and when I spoke out against it I was marginalized and vilified. Then the dream breaks to another scene and I'm being interviewed on a national news show, and the interviewer asks me if I believe Homosexuality is a Sin. I said; Let me ask you, DO YOU BELIEVE THE BIBLE SIR? Are you a Spiritual man? He hesitates. So I say, well if you're not a spiritual man, you seem like an intelligent man. So answer this question and I'll answer yours. And if you can educate me intellectually on this subject, I'll do my best to inform you biblically. "IS HOMOSEXUALITY NATURAL?" Is it natural for a man to stick his "giving instrument," or any other instrument for that matter, into a hole that was made to give out "Refuse?" In the dream the interviewer was flustered, saying; in our country everybody has a right to do what they want, as long as it doesn't harm others. I agreed! But I asked again, Is it NATURAL? He refused to answer me. So I would not answer him.

Then I woke up. When I awoke I started my devotions, reading my daily bible reading plan. Guess where it took me? Leviticus 18; the chapter that speaks against having sexual relations with the same kin, and then, the same sex, as well as with animals. It dawned on me reading that whole chapter that our society has legitimized same sex relations, but still view same kin sexual relations as unnatural. How long will it be before we legitimize same kin relations?

> **Lev 18:1** And the LORD spoke to Moses, saying, 2 "Speak to the people of Israel and say to them, I am the LORD your God. 3 You shall not do as they do in the land of Egypt, where you lived, and you shall not do as they do in the land of Canaan, to which I am bringing you. You shall not walk in their statutes. 4 You shall follow my rules

and keep my statutes and walk in them. I am the LORD your God. 5 You shall therefore keep my statutes and my rules; if a person does them, he shall live by them: I am the LORD. 6"None of you shall approach any one of his close relatives to uncover nakedness. I am the LORD.

7 You shall not uncover the nakedness of your father, which is the nakedness of your mother; she is your mother, you shall not uncover her nakedness. 8 You shall not uncover the nakedness of your father's wife; it is your father's nakedness. 9 You shall not uncover the nakedness of your sister, your father's daughter or your mother's daughter, whether brought up in the family or in another home. 10 You shall not uncover the nakedness of your son's daughter or of your daughter's daughter, for their nakedness is your own nakedness.

11 You shall not uncover the nakedness of your father's wife's daughter, brought up in your father's family, since she is your sister. 12 You shall not uncover the nakedness of your father's sister; she is your father's relative. 13 You shall not uncover the nakedness of your mother's sister, for she is your mother's relative. 14 You shall not uncover the nakedness of your father's brother, that is, you shall not approach his wife; she is your aunt.

15 You shall not uncover the nakedness of your daughter-in-law; she is your son's wife, you shall not uncover her nakedness. 16 You shall not uncover the nakedness of your brother's wife; it is your brother's nakedness. 17 You shall not uncover the nakedness of a woman and of her daughter, and you shall not take her son's daughter or her daughter's daughter to uncover her nakedness; they are relatives; it is depravity.

Lev 18:18 and you shall not take a woman as a rival wife to her sister, uncovering her nakedness while her sister is still alive. 19 "You shall not approach a woman to uncover her nakedness while she is in her menstrual uncleanness. 20 And you shall not lie sexually with your neighbor's wife and so make yourself unclean with her. 21. You shall not give any of your children to offer them to Molech, and so profane the name of your God: I am the LORD. 22 You shall not lie *with a male as with a woman; it is an abomination. 23 And you shall not lie with any animal and so make yourself unclean with it, neither shall any woman give herself to an animal to lie with it: it is perversion. 24 "Do not make yourselves unclean by any of these things, for by all these the nations I am driving out before you have become unclean, 25 and the land became unclean, so that I punished its iniquity, and the land vomited out its inhabitants.*

26 But you shall keep my statutes and my rules and do none of these abominations, either the native or the stranger who sojourns among you 27 (for the people of the land, who were before you, did all of these abominations, so that the land became unclean), 28 lest the land vomit you out when you make it unclean, as it vomited out the nation that was before you. 29 For everyone who does any of these abominations, the persons who do them shall be cut off from among their people. 30 So keep my charge never to practice any of these abominable customs that were practiced before you, and never to make yourselves unclean by them: I am the LORD your God."

After I finished reading Leviticus 18, I felt an urge to post my dream and scripture from Leviticus 18 on Facebook. I received various responses back in the comment thread. Below is one response to this dream and my interpretation of the dream explained to this respondent.

> **Facebook respondent**: I personally don't believe it is my right as a human being, let alone a Christian to try to change what they feel like is a natural desire. I feel like it is simply my duty to love my neighbor, gay or straight. Even logically speaking, it is highly unlikely and even ridiculous to think a gay man will "stop" being gay after conversations with me. It should be done by the Holy Spirit. No one can come to the father unless drawn by the spirit right?
>
> Your dream, though compelling in thought, won't work with this generation. At least from my uneducated opinion. They'll turn away from you before even hearing your argument. We long for sincerity and community, not for church language ideologies. I apologize if I misread or misunderstood something.

Brondon Mathis: Sir it sounds like you missed the essence of the dreams interpretation.

And while I wasn't sure of all God was revealing in the dream at the time, I've been receiving more and more each day with my dialogue with the Lord, and with every comment posted.

So here's what I got from the dream. # 1. I sensed through the actions of these men at the bus stop I was being challenged to speak up to let them know that I was uncomfortable with their public display of affection. I put in parenthesis that I would feel uncomfortable with heterosexual PDA. Challenge #1 Brondon will you speak out against this issue of unlawful sexuality in your society (at every level and in all forms. (*Lev 18 doesn't just speak against same sex relations being unlawful but same kin, etc.*) Sir, I didn't sense from this part of the dream that I was trying to change a homosexual. But I sensed God was challenging me, "Will you speak up that not only is what you're doing not right, but I'm not comfortable with it." Will you raise up a standard that this is wrong in a generation that is saying its right or alright. The first step to getting an individual to a place of freedom in any area is to know the truth about what they are doing, that it's not right or natural. If a person thinks what they're doing is right or alright why would they want to stop or be set free?

#2. In the second part of the dream I felt like God was showing me how to speak out against unlawful sexuality. Don't try to speak theologically to a generation that doesn't believe the bible, or that doesn't believe the bible is our moral authority. Jesus said, except a man is born again he cannot see the kingdom of God. (John 3:3). We must appeal naturally to a generation that is completely adverse and antagonistic to our biblical beliefs of morality and ethics. We must meet them where they are on their level, with the wisdom and love of God. Notice Sir in the second scene of the dream the interviewer was questioning me about my biblical beliefs, about whether homosexuality was sin. At that point I was not trying to change a homosexual, nor was I trying to reach a homosexual. I was actually being put on trial with the question as to whether my response would warrant me being marginalized as a preacher of hate or at the least someone who should be silenced and ignored in a society that so desperately needs voices of reason and compassion. In that part of the dream I felt like God was showing me when to speak out, how to speak out and when not to speak out. But notice I wasn't speaking to a homosexual, which I could tell in the dream, trying to get him to change. I was speaking to an intellectual trying to show him intellectually why homosexuality is wrong. Not just that it is sin because the bible says so, but it's wrong because it's not natural. It's not how our bodies were made us to intimately interact or relate. Therefore it's unlawful because it's unnatural.

#3 finally, with the chapter in Leviticus I believe God was showing me the inevitable destiny of a society that starts on the road of accepting and legitimizing the immoral act of same sex relations. Next is same kin relations. Then its relations with animals. And lastly the land is defiled and God will visit the iniquity upon it, vomiting up its inhabitants.

So Sir as I saw the dream, it was less about trying to reach a generation of homosexuals to get them to change and more about trying to reach a society that is increasingly embracing this lifestyle as being alright, or a generation that has lost its moral senses and believes that all sexual immorality is alright. And if its' alright or natural, no one should speak out against it. The dream was more about whose going speak up and say this is wrong. And how do you speak up and say this is wrong, with wisdom and prudence. When do you speak up and say it's wrong, in a way when those that are listening can receive it? And why is it necessary to speak up and say its' wrong?

Because if we don't our society will slide down the scale from human behavior to animal behavior to societal extinction.

My Testimony of Why I Can't Receive the Philosophy and Morality Standard of the Gay Agenda

Personally for me, the number one reason I cannot agree with or receive the philosophy and morality standard of this generation's gay agenda that's being propagated, is not as much my biblical defense of biblical sexuality, as much as it is my personal defense of my family, my wife and children. Let me explain. As I stated in Chapter 1, when I was a teenager I was awakened to my sexual desires by a movie called, *The Postman always rings twice.* This was my first presentation of passionate, erotic sexual acts, as a wife was being unfaithful to her husband with a Postman. This sexual presentation marked me as a 14 year old boy. It marked me and seared several images on my sexual DNA. The first image that it seared was that sex outside of marriage was something that was especially erotic, and more desirable than sex with your own husband or wife. Another image that it seared upon my sexual DNA was that sex with White women was especially erotic and more desirable than sex with other races. As a black man in the 1970's and the early 1980's I rarely saw images of black women on TV that presented beauty and eloquence with women of color. Therefore, I grew up with a special attraction to and desire to be with White women sexually.

These two desires shaped my sexual DNA. This encounter with this movie, in my teens, was the earliest entry point for this shaping of my sexual DNA. There was a problem however, I was raised in a Christian home that presented biblically sexually as sex only in the context of marriage. However, our society was in the midst of a 20 year sexual revolution from the 1960's of free and open sex with anybody, whether they were your spouse or not, whether you knew them or not. Everything was permitted and okay. When I became sexually active this was my grapple and propensity - a society that promoted free and open sex, verses my biblical foundation of sex in the context of marriage as the standard of sexual morality.

From 19 years old when I first became sexually active, to the time I got married, I struggled with my society and generation's presentation of sex and my Christian upbringing's presentation of sex – between one man and woman in the context of the marriage covenant. I had multiple experiences with several women outside of the marriage covenant, with the majority of them being white women. I didn't feel anything bad about those women being white, because by that time it was more accepted in society. My main struggle was with sex outside of marriage. As a result I was very perplexed in my soul relationally. Many of my Christian friends were getting married between the ages of 22 and 28 years old, having kept themselves from sexual activity and they were developing strong, healthy relationships, while I was having casual encounters with women that never lasted past 3 to 6 months, and was always toxic and surface, with sex being the only basis for our relationship. Between 22 – 25 years old, I re-committed my life to Jesus Christ and His presentation of biblical sexuality and morality. I made a commitment not to have sex again until I was married, and I made a commitment to love with all my heart whoever God connected my heart with, not my flesh, whether they were White, Black, or Asian. I still struggled with wanting to have casual sex with White women, but I would always come back to my commitment to God and myself. Finally at 29 years of age, I met my wife Noe Williams, a beautiful tanned Black woman that has some Indian and Caucasian in her family lineage. We were married on Oct 21 1995, and have five children, 3 girls and 2 boys.

Now on to the reason I can't afford to agree with the philosophy and moral standard of this generation's presentation of sexuality and morality. As a married man, I still have to resist my former sexual appetites that were established in my sexual DNA as a teenager. I'm still attracted to women that are not my wife. I'm still especially attracted to White women. I know this is going to sound harsh, but it's the truth, and it's my reality. I'm not tempted as much by beautiful black women. I recognize the beauty in Black women, but because the majority of my sexual experiences before marriage were with White women, my main temptation that I must resist is with the presentation with beautiful White women. However, because I love my wife and my kids, and because I love my God and his ways that are laid out in the word of God, for His standard of success and morality, I say NO to those presentations that come my way, because I'm married with 5 kids.

The Gay agenda premise, that because this is their sexual preference and orientation they should have a right to do what they feel and be with whoever they want to be with, besides the fact that this is not the morality standard our generation was founded upon, this is not advantageous to my wife and family, for me to accept this standard of morality. It opens me up to follow my own sexual orientation and presentation of sex outside of marriage, to be with any and every woman that my flesh desires. The same way I and any other married men have to say NO to their sexual dictates that have been established in their sexual DNA, however they were established, whether as a teenager, an adolescence, or in the womb, the proper designation and presentation of sexuality and morality that this civilization was built upon was a man with a woman, in the context of marriage. This is the standard for humanity, whether we fall short of it or not. Just because we miss the mark out of our moral decline and decay as a society, is no reason to change or remove the standard. We have to keep seeking to measure up to this standard placed in humanity by the grace of God and resist any presentation that would threaten the construct of our civilization that was established and built for the longevity and eternal existence of humanity in the earth.

Intolerance or Love

For all those that want to call me intolerant because I have standards of right and wrong sexually, I have this answer: In any civil society there must be standards of right and wrong, morality and immorality. And there must be some kind of infallible document that this standard comes from. For me and for our civilization, for the last 3-5 millenniums, that document has been the Bible. It's not an issue of intolerance, it's actually an issue of love and grace. There can be no love or grace without a standard of righteousness and morality that mankind falls short of. You only need and qualify for God's love and grace when you recognize your sin, and your need to be loved unconditionally in your sin and unrighteousness, which will eventually empower you to desire to come out of your sin and unrighteousness. John 3:16 does not say "God so loved the angels, or GOD so loved Perfect Christians, but it says, God so loved the World - *Those that were separated from Him because of Adams sin, to which we were all born in.* WE WERE ALL BORN THIS WAY! We were all born in some sin issue that causes us to live short of our original righteousness nature. God so LOVED us that He gave Jesus - grace to die in our place - that whoever believes and receives him doesn't have to die the way they were born.

Chapter 11

A PRAYER ENCOUNTER WITH THE GLORIFIED CHRIST TO OVERCOME THE JEZEBEL SPIRIT

Mar 9:2 And after six days Jesus taketh with him Peter, and James, and John, and leadeth them up into an high mountain apart by themselves: and he was transfigured before them. 3 And his raiment became shining, exceeding white as snow; so as no fuller on earth can white them. 4. And there appeared unto them Elias with Moses: and they were talking with Jesus.

Luk 9:28 And it came to pass about an eight days after these sayings, he took Peter and John and James, and went up into a mountain to pray. 29 And as he prayed, the fashion of his countenance was altered, and his raiment was white and glistering. 30 And, behold, there talked with him two men, which were Moses and Elias: 31 Who appeared in glory, and spake of his decease which he should accomplish at Jerusalem. But Peter and they that were with him were heavy with sleep: and when they were awake, they saw his glory, and the two men that stood with him.

From these passages in Mark 9 and Luke 9 we can see that when Jesus said that this kind of power can only be released by prayer, he was talking about an Encounter in prayer with a person. He was speaking about prayer that encounters the beauty of the glorified Christ and sees the beauty and glory of God in prayer. This type of prayer is what it takes to overcome the jezebel spirit, with all her witchcrafts, sorcery and whoredoms (*Prostitution, faithless, unworthy, idolatrous practices or pursuits*). The problem is, it's this very practice of prayer that's missing in the modern church of our generation. Therefore this type of power to overcome Jezebels whoredoms is missing from the church of this generation. Paul records a glory encounter with the glorified Christ that empowered him to do all that God had called him to do in the earth in Acts 26:13-18.

> *Act 26:13 At midday, O king, I saw in the way a light from heaven, above the brightness of the sun, shining round about me and them which journeyed with me. 14 And when we were all fallen to the earth, I heard a voice speaking unto me, and saying in the Hebrew tongue, Saul, Saul, why persecutest thou me? it is hard for thee to kick against the pricks. 15 And I said, Who art thou, Lord? And he said, I am Jesus whom thou persecutest. 16 But rise, and stand upon thy feet: for I have appeared unto thee for this purpose, to make thee a minister and a witness both of these things which thou hast seen, and of those things in the which I will appear unto thee; 17 Delivering thee from the people, and from the Gentiles, unto whom now I send thee, 18 To open their eyes, and to turn them from darkness to light, and from the power of Satan unto God, that they may receive forgiveness of sins, and inheritance among them which are sanctified by faith that is in me.*

Paul goes on to say as a result of this encounter:

> *Whereupon, O king Agrippa, I was not disobedient unto the heavenly vision. (Acts 26:19)*

How did Paul have the power to fulfill the Heavenly vision? Paul had a visitation from Heaven. Paul encountered the Glorified Christ. Therefore he had the power to overcome every opposition to his call, to do all that God had commissioned him to do. Our Power to do and be all that God has called us to do and be is found in an encounter with the Glorified Christ.

In Psalm 27:4 *David said, one thing Have I desired of the Lord...to behold the beauty of the Lord*. Again in our generation, as in David's, the Holy Spirit is orchestrating a worldwide worship movement that is essential in releasing God's beauty and power in the nations. The power of God is not just going to break out, and then, suddenly the power to overcome Jezebel and reap the great harvest will happen. Before the second coming, God's power is going to break out, in relation to a global prayer and worship movement. It is happening right now; it is all over the world.

Here is the key point: this movement is fueled by the revelation of encountering the beauty of God. David's prayer ministry was fueled by this revelation of encountering the beauty of God. Towards this end David had 4,000 musicians who were full-time singers that worshipped 24/7 committed to this – Beholding (encountering) the Beauty of the Lord. Lord raise up your singers, worshipers & intercessors in an end-time day and night prayer and worship movement committed to beholding your beauty. If we're going to see the power in prayer to overcome the spirit of Jezebel, and her immorality surge from hell at the end of the age, we must seek and receive an encounter with God in prayer. God spoke to my heart one day in prayer and said, "**Brondon, when I am your reward in prayer, I will reward your prayers with Power.**"

God told Abraham something similar to this in Genesis 15:1, saying, *I am thy great reward.*

> *"After these things the word of the LORD came unto Abram in a vision, saying, Fear not, Abram: I am thy shield, and thy exceeding great reward.*

God wants to be our reward in prayer, his very presence, his very person, him showing us His glory, as we seek his face, not his hand. Psalm 24:6 David said this glory encounter generation would be characterized by a generation that seeks him, that seeks his face. This was also Moses prayer and heart after God. Moses was actually the first to desire a glory, beauty encounter in Psalm 90 praying in verse 17 "may the beauty of the Lord our God rests upon us; establish the work of our hands for us, yea the work of our hands establish thou it. And in Exodus 33:13-15 Moses prayed;

> *Now therefore, I pray thee, if I have found grace in thy sight, shew me now thy way, that I may know thee, that I may find grace in thy sight: and consider that this nation is thy people. And he said, My presence shall go*

with thee, and I will give you rest. ***And he said unto him, If thy presence go not with me, carry us not up hence.* Exo. 33:13-15**

And let the beauty of the LORD our God be upon us: and establish thou the work of our hands upon us; yea, the work of our hands establish thou it. **Psa. 90:17**

Encountering the Brightness of God's Beauty in His Son

When He is our reward in prayer he will reward our prayers with Power and Beauty. When we encounter his beauty in prayer he will establish the work of our hands. The Spirit of Jezebel wants to attract a generation that's destined to behold true beauty, and give them a false presentation of perverted beauty through pornography and sexual immorality to destroy their senses from ever appreciating and pursuing the beauty of God. Psalm 45 talks about that true beauty that is our inheritance, and what it looks like and what our response will be to His beauty.

Psalm 45: 1 Beautiful thoughts fill my mind as I speak these lines for the king. These words come from my tongue as from the pen of a skilled writer. ***2 Thou art fairer than the children of men: grace is poured into thy lips: therefore God hath blessed thee forever.*** *3 Gird thy sword upon thy thigh, O most mighty, with thy glory and thy majesty.* ***4 And in thy majesty ride prosperously because of truth and meekness and righteousness; and thy right hand shall teach thee terrible things.*** *5 Thine arrows are sharp in the heart of the king's enemies; whereby the people fall under thee. 6 Thy throne, O God, is for ever and ever: the sceptre of thy kingdom is a right sceptre.* ***<u>7 You love righteousness, and hate wickedness: therefore God, thy God, hath anointed thee with the oil of gladness above thy fellows. 8 All thy garments smell of myrrh, and aloes, and cassia, out of the ivory palaces, whereby they have made thee</u>*** *glad. 9 Kings' daughters were among thy honorable women: upon thy right hand did stand the queen in gold of Ophir. 10 Hearken, O daughter, and consider, and incline thine ear; forget also thine own people, and thy father's house;* ***<u>11 So shall the king greatly desire thy beauty: for he is thy Lord; and worship thou him.</u>***

These verses prophetically speak of the beauty of Jesus the Messiah. And how to get true beauty on our minds and hearts, in place of the perverted beauty and thoughts of the fallen world. Psa. 45:1 is a love song, the words of which, the more you speak, the more these words write his beauty on our mental hard drive, and renews our minds to true beauty. Psalm 45:2 tells us how much more beautiful He is than the children of men, (those born into the earth after Adam's sin), and what this beauty looks like. **Verse 2 says, You (Jesus) are fairer (more beautiful) than the children of Men.**

His Beauty is More Beautiful than the Beauty of Man

The word "*fairer*" is the Hebrew word "*Yaw Faw*" which means to be *bright, and beautiful.* There's a difference between beauty that is bright and full of light, and beauty that dark and full of sin. Beauty that is bright is radiant as the sun, bringing light, or illumination and revelation to man's spirit concerning the beauty of God and His awesome purpose for humanity to behold His beauty and become like Him. Beauty that is dark and full of sin, detracts from man, and His ability to access the revelation of the beauty of God and God's true purpose for humanity in beholding Him. Perverted beauty found in sexual immorality and perversion releases a darkness that is synonymous with ignorance or a lack of knowledge. The beauty of God that is so much more and fairer than the children of men is rooted in the revelation of the Word of God. Verse 2 goes on to say, that **grace is poured into thy lips, therefore, God becomes your God and blesses thee forever.** The Hebrew word for "grace" is the word "chen" (Khane) which means; *graciousness, that is, subjectively (kindness, favor) or objectively (beauty): - favor, grace (-ious), pleasant, precious, [well-] favored.* The Beauty of God is transmitted into our hearts and minds when we speak of the things concerning the King. (v.1)

Psalm 45:4 goes on to describe the characteristics of this beauty of God's son as being **Truth**, **Meekness** and **Righteousness**. This beauty is manifest in man's spiritual eye, not in the physical eye, causing man to hate wickedness and loves righteousness. The more revelation we receive of the truth of who Jesus is, His meekness, and righteousness, the more we will love righteousness and hate wickedness. The reason why we tolerate wickedness and compromise the true beauty of God's

Son for the perverted of beauty of pornography or immorality, is because we have never received a revelation encounter with the truth, meekness and righteousness of the Beauty of God's Son. These three beauty agents reveal what true beauty looks like and how to replace the dark Beauty of pornography, sexual perversion, immorality, lust, anger, malice, hatred, murder, and the like, with the Beauty that is light, that brings illumination and revelation of the nature of the beauty of God.

The Beauty of Christ's Truth

And in thy majesty ride prosperously because of truth – Psa. 45:4

The words majesty, and prosperously give us keys to unlocking the beauty of God's truth, meekness and righteousness. <u>The word "majesty"</u> in the Hebrew is the word; *hâdâr (haw-dawr)* which means; **magnificence, that is, ornament or splendor: - beauty, comeliness, excellency, glorious, glory, goodly, honour, majesty**.

<u>The word "prosperously"</u> in the Hebrew is the word; tsâlach tsâlêach (tsaw-lakh', tsaw-lay'-akh) which means; **to push forward, in various senses (literally or figuratively, transitively or intransitively): - break out, come (mightily), go over, be good, be meet, be profitable, (cause to, effect, make to, send) prosper (-ity, -ous, -ously)**.

The Beauty of God comes from the Truth of God, the meekness of God and the righteousness of God. This beauty of God's truth, meekness and righteousness breaks through the darkness of the perverted beauty of this world when we allow the truth to be the carrier or establishment of what's reality, as opposed to what society places before us as reality. *And in thy majesty (beauty)* <u>ride prosperously</u> *because of truth, meekness, and righteousness.*

<u>The word "ride"</u> in the Hebrew is the word; râkab (raw-kab) which means; **to ride (on an animal or in a vehicle); causatively to place upon (for riding or generally), to despatch: - bring (on [horse-] back), carry, get [oneself] up, on [horse-] back, put, (cause to, make to) ride (in a chariot, on, -r), set**.

When we allow the truth of God's word to be the carrier of reality into our hearts and minds, God's beauty will break out in our soul as the preeminence of beauty in our hearts.

Truth - in the Hebrew the word truth is **"eh'-meth"** *Contracted from (aw-man'- A primitive root; properly to build up or support; to foster as a parent or nurse; figuratively to render (or be) firm or faithful, to trust or believe, to be permanent or quiet; morally to be true or certain; once (in Isa_30:21; by interchange for H541) to go to the right hand: - hence assurance, believe, bring up, establish, + fail be faithful (of long continuance, stedfast, sure, surely, trusty, verified), nurse, (-ing father), (put), trust, turn to the right.) stability; figurctively certainty, truth, trustworthiness: - assured (-ly), establishment, faithful, right, sure, true (-ly, -th), verity.*

What is Truth? This is what Pilate asked Jesus in John 18:38

Joh 18:37 *Pilate therefore said unto him, Art thou a king then? Jesus answered, Thou sayest that I am a king. To this end was I born, and for this cause came I into the world, that I should bear witness unto the truth. Every one that is of the truth heareth my voice. 38* **Pilate saith unto him, What is truth?**

Joh 14:6 Jesus saith unto him, I am the way, **the truth**, *and the life: no man cometh unto the Father, but by me.*

Jesus called his way to life the truth. He said He was the way to the truth that will lead mankind to true beauty. The way speaks of the road by which Jesus arrived to the place of the reconciliation of the world back to God to which God so loved. That way to God's beauty is through the road of meekness.

The Beauty of Christ's Meekness

Meekness – in the Hebrew the word - is *an-vaw' Feminine of H6035; mildness (royal); also (concretely) oppressed: - gentleness, meekness.* **aw-nawv', aw-nawv'** *The second form is by intermixture with H6041; from H6031; depressed (figuratively), in mind (gentle) or circumstances (needy, especially saintly): - humble, lowly, meek, poor.*
The way to this beauty of God in meekness can be summed in Phil. 2:1-8

Php 2:1 If there be therefore any consolation in Christ, if any comfort of love, if any fellowship of the Spirit, if any bowels and mercies, 2 Fulfil ye my joy, that ye be likeminded, having the same love, being of one accord, of one mind. 3 Let nothing be done through strife or vainglory; but in lowliness of mind let each esteem other better than themselves.

4 Look not every man on his own things, but every man also on the things of others. 5 Let this mind be in you, which was also in Christ Jesus: 6 Who, being in the form of God, thought it not robbery to be equal with God: 7 But made himself of no reputation, and took upon him the form of a servant, and was made in the likeness of men:

8 And being found in fashion as a man, he humbled himself, and became obedient unto death, even the death of the cross. 9 Wherefore God also hath highly exalted him, and given him a name which is above every name:

The Beauty of Christ's Righteousness

Righteousness - *From A primitive root tsaw-dak; meaning to be (causatively make) right (in a moral or forensic sense): - cleanse, clear self, (be, do) just (-ice, -ify, -ify self), (be, turn to) righteous (-ness).; the right (natural, moral or legal); also (abstractly) equity or (figuratively) prosperity: - X even, (X that which is altogether) just (-ice), ([un-]) right (-eous) (cause, -ly, -ness)*

John Piper explains how the beauty of God is better than man's lust, and how we can overcome the lust of porn addiction by the Beauties of God, in his article entitled; **No One is Absolutely Addicted to Pornography**

John Piper, founder of Desiring God (Facebook)

Not all sexual desire is lust. God made sexual desire. It has its good place and it can, in fact, become an act of worship in the temple of marriage. But lust is sexual desire gone wrong. Here's my definition:

Lust is a sexual desire that dishonors its object and disregards God. Disregards the promises and the warnings of having or losing the beauties of Christ.

The lusted-after woman or man in your head, or on the screen, or on the street, is dishonored—not treated as a sacred, precious, eternal person made in the image of God, whose eternal destiny is always paramount, and whose holiness we either long for or ignore. And the only way this dishonor can be so daringly carried out is by disregarding God while we are in the sway of our lust—disregarding the promises and warnings of having or losing the beauties of Christ. So lust is a sexual desire that dishonors its object and disregards God. Ponder with me for a few minutes the natural and the spiritual role of self-control in relation to lust.

Faith in Christ Conquers 'Addiction'

Addiction is a relative term. I would stake my life on the assumption that no one in this room is absolutely addicted to pornography or any sexual sin. What I mean is this: If the stakes are high enough and sure enough, you will have all the self-control you need to resist any sexual temptation.

For example, if tonight you are feeling totally in the sway of sexual desire—more blazing, more powerful than you have ever felt it in your life—and you believe that you cannot resist the temptation to look at some nudity online, and suddenly a black-hooded ISIS member drags your best friend or your spouse into the room with a knife at his or her throat, and says, "If you look at that website, I will slit their throat," you will have the self-control you thought you didn't have. You won't click.

Or if a man walks into the room and says, "If you do not look at that nudity, I will give you $1 million cash, tax-free, tonight," you will suddenly have the self-control you thought you did not have.

Addiction is a relative term. The fact is, 99 percent of those who give way to lust in pornography or fornication or adultery, are not decisively controlled by sexual desire. They are decisively controlled by what they believe—what they believe will happen if they act on their lust or don't.

The Spirit of God Controls Us

The decisive issue is whether they believe the stakes are high enough and sure enough. If we are sure a friend will die a gruesome death, we will have self-control. If we are sure we'll get the $1 million we will have self-control.

Now there is nothing distinctly Christian about that analysis of motivation. That is simply the way human beings are wired. Self-control was a Stoic virtue before it was Christian, and there is nothing distinctly Christian about it.

And yet Paul lists self-control (engkrateia) as a fruit of the Spirit (Gal. 5:23). So for those who believe the gospel of Christ, and are justified by faith alone (Rom. 3:28), the Holy Spirit becomes the decisive cause of "self-control." That's what I take "fruit" to mean in Galatians 5. The Spirit produces self-control in the believer. The action of the self is vital and essential, but not decisive. The Spirit is decisive.

Work out your salvation for God is at work in you, Paul says in Philippians 2:12–13. That means "Control your lusts because the Spirit is controlling them through you." Exert self-control, because the Spirit is working it in you. The blood of Christ, the blood of the new covenant, secures for us the working of the Holy Spirit. And when He works, we act. His working appears in our acting. He creates the miracle of self-control, and we act the miracle of self-control.

But the Holy Spirit doesn't produce the same self-control that the Stoics had. The Stoics did not depend on Christ, or live for Christ. But the Holy Spirit is in the believer because of the death of Christ, and for the glory of Christ (John 14:16). The blood of Christ was His price. And the beauty of Christ is His mission.

The Beauty of Christ Is Better

Therefore, the way the Spirit produces self-control in the believer is by revealing the beauties of Christ to our souls as supremely beautiful and supremely satisfying. He removes the hardness of heart and the blindness of our souls, so that we see and savor the beauties of Christ for what they really are.

And what He shows us through the Word of Christ is that the all-satisfying beauties of Christ can be lost forever, if in the bondage of lust we prove to be a hypocrite and really love sex more than we love Christ. And he shows us that the day is coming, and now is here in measure, when we will enjoy Christ with a fullness of joy that outweighs every possible pleasure of lust.

Which brings us back now to the ISIS member ready to slit the throat of our best friend, and the man with a million dollars. The Holy Spirit shows us that the stakes are much higher than either of those situations when we face the temptations of lust. These beauties of Christ that the Holy Spirit reveals can be lost forever, or they can satisfy your soul forever.

He opens our ears to hear Jesus say, "If your right eye causes you to sin, tear it out and throw it away. For it is better that you lose one of your members than that your whole body be thrown into hell" (Matt. 5:29)—the final and ultimate ISIS attack. And He opens our ears to hear Jesus say, "Blessed are the pure in heart, for they shall see God" (Matt. 5:8)—a reward infinitely superior to a mere million dollars.

Self-control is a fruit of the Spirit. He creates the miracle. We act the miracle. He creates it by opening our eyes to see the beauties of Christ— that they can be lost forever in bondage to lust, or enjoyed forever by the pure in heart.

John Piper (@JohnPiper) *is founder and teacher of desiringgod.org and chancellor of Bethlehem College & Seminary. For 33 years, he served as pastor of Bethlehem Baptist Church, Minneapolis, Minnesota. He is author of more than 50 books.*

This article was used with permission from desiringgod.org.

The Prayer Climb up the Mountain of Encounter

Power in prayer to see the beauties of God and overcome lust comes with the invitation of Jesus in Mark 9:3 to encounter the glorified Christ. *After so many days Jesus took Peter, James and John and led them up a high mountain to pray*. If we're going to have an encounter with Jesus there are several things that we must focus on from these passages in Mark and Luke as we follow Jesus up the mountain to encounter:

1. We must let him "**take us**," all of us. WE MUST BE TAKEN BY HIM, spirit, soul and body. This verse said, "*After so many days Jesus **took** Peter, James and John*...What does it take to be taken by Jesus? It is the Greek word – para lam banō - which means -*to receive near, that is, associate with oneself (in any familiar or intimate act or relation); by analogy to assume an office; figuratively to learn: - receive, take (unto, with)*. We must associate ourselves with Jesus in an intimate way that we might be completely and totally obedient to him, doing all he tells us to do, totally surrendered. When we get to the place where we are letting Jesus take us we're on our way to an encounter with the glorified Christ.

2. Next after he takes us we must let him **lead us**. When we are taken by Jesus he's able to lead us to a place in prayer that is guided by him. We don't encounter him in prayer because we don't let him lead us in prayer. We don't let him lead our prayers. Romans 8:26 says, *we don't*

know what we should pray for as we ought; but the spirit himself makes intercession for us with groanings that cannot be uttered. We want to pray about everything else but what he wants us to pray about. But when he leads us in prayer we will be directed in our prayers to pray what he wants, not what we want. The Greek word for to "lead up" is a word *"an-af-er-o,"* which means to offer up. We must let him offer us up that our prayers will be received and answered in the earth. Our prayer life must be a sacrificial offering up of our lives and bodies to him that we might be vessels unto honor that he can pray his will through for the earth.

3. When we let him lead us in prayer, He will lead us up into the mountain of prayer. **We must enter into the mountain of prayer, which represents the spirit world, to receive the power of prayer.** The text said, "*He led them up into a high mountain to* **pray**". To come into the mountain of prayer is more than a place of saying a prayer recital. Going into a mountain to pray is symbolic of going from one kingdom into another kingdom for an extended time in the presence of God. Mountains in scripture represent kingdoms. When he leads us up into a mountain he's taking us from one world, the natural world in prayer, to the spirit world in prayer. This is not a quick thing that we can do in a minute or an hour, but we need an extended time of prayer. When Jesus went up into a mountain to pray he was usually there all night in prayer. Isaiah 56:7 says, Even them shall I bring to my holy mountain, and I will make them joyful in my house of prayer. The house of prayer paradigm is all about the church becoming joyful in the end-time mission of prayer. When we become joyful in the house of prayer we will become a mighty mountain in the earth. When we become a house of prayer all the nations will flow into his Holy Mountain. Isaiah 2:2-5 says:

> ***Isa 2:2*** *And it shall come to pass in the last days, that the mountain of the LORD'S house shall be established in the top of the mountains, and shall be exalted above the hills; and all nations shall flow unto it. 3 And many people shall go and say, Come ye, and let us go up to the mountain of the LORD, to the house of the God of Jacob; and he will teach us of his ways, and we will walk in his paths: for out of Zion shall go forth the law, and the*

> *word of the LORD from Jerusalem. 4 And he shall judge among the nations, and shall rebuke many people: and they shall beat their swords into plowshares, and their spears into pruninghooks: nation shall not lift up sword against nation, neither shall they learn war any more. 5 O house of Jacob, come ye, and let us walk in the light of the LORD.*

We won't encounter God in prayer without letting him have our lives, our bodies and our time, letting him have a set aside time of hours, days, and seasons of prayer. Until we let Jesus take us up into the mountain of prayer for extended seasons of prayer by the spirit we will not encounter him. And No encounter, No power.

Alone on the Mountain with the Glorified Christ

Again in Mark 9:4 it says when they were all alone, there he was transfigured before them. His clothes became dazzling white, whiter than anyone in the world could bleach them. And there appeared before them Elijah, and Moses who were talking with Jesus. I heard a preacher say once, "We must learn to get alone with God until we're not alone anymore." When they got alone with God for an extended season of prayer they were no longer alone anymore. They began to see the Glorified Christ, the eternal Christ that was before the world began, conversing with Elijah and Moses. I believe this represents the power of the spirit that's coming from an end-time encounter with Jesus in prayer in the days to come. I believe in the end time prayer movement God is releasing the power of the spirit of Elijah and Moses back to our churches and prayer meetings, and like Elijah against Jezebels prophets, and Moses against Pharaoh, we will be delivered from the Spirit of Jezebel, and the system she's has placed in the earth.

CHAPTER 12

THE PURITY STAND OF PHINEHAS

Num 25:13 And he shall have it, and his seed after him, even the covenant of an everlasting priesthood; because he was zealous for his God, and made an atonement for the children of Israel.

In receiving deliverance from the spirit of Jezebel and leading others into this victory the pathway requires purity and holiness and the stand of Phinehas. Christ-ones that lead at the end of the age are going to have to confront immorality and sexual perversion that will be released in the earth in unprecedented measures. The fourfold increase of evil at the end of the age will include murder, sorcery, fornication and theft.

Rev 9:21 Neither repented they of their murders, nor of their sorceries, nor of their fornication, nor of their thefts.

These are all characteristic traits of the Jezebel spirit. If this generation of believers are going to be raised up again to lead others into victory over the spirit of Jezebel we're going to have to see the curse of iniquity reversed that has been on us because of sexual immorality, and see the release of blessing and peace to break us free from Jezebel.

Breaking the Cycle of Past Generations of Immorality

The final generations are going to have to raise the standard of Holiness and purity in order to confront this increased release of the spirit of immorality in the earth as seen coming at the end of the age from the above verse from Revelation 9:21. Unfortunately in past generations this spirit took down many ministers, ministries and kingdoms that sought to walk in fullness as they prepared the way for the coming of the Lord in the earth. Much can be said about those that were confronted with the spirit of Jezebel and tolerated this spirit in past generations. Great men of God from generations past both from scripture and beyond like, David to Solomon, to Dr. Martin Luther King Jr. were all confronted with this spirit of Jezebel and at times compromised with grave consequences. It is well documented in the scripture, as well as in the history books, the failures and compromises of these great men from past generations in the area of sexual purity. And while I don't believe their failures in the areas of sexual purity can abdicate or nullify their great victories that were wrought through their lives, nor the honor that we bestow upon them, I do believe that David, Solomon and many of the great men in history were not able to see and come to the place of the fullness of their desires in God during their lifetimes because of these moral failures. Dr. King acknowledged at the end of his life, I'm not going to get to see all I've worked to see, or all I've desired to see, as he stated the night before he passed. As he eloquently declared, I've been to the mountaintop, and I've seen the promised-land. I may not get there with you.... Realizing that there was a place, like Moses, he desired to arrive to, but like Moses, God would take him right outside of the promise. He didn't reach fullness.

We must come to see that there's more to reach for in God that the past generations of leaders didn't attain unto. And in the reaching for these mountaintops our purity and morality will often times be the difference between going to the top and seeing the promise and going over into the fullness of everything God has for this generation. If this generation is going to lead the church in the earth to the end of the age and cross us over into all that God has for us, we're going to have to resist the spirit of Jezebel, which leads to moral failure in the area of sexual purity. Solomon left us many wise and noble writings in scripture but in the latter years of his life he compromised greatly with sexual immorality with over 700 wives and many more concubines from foreign nations that served idol gods. These women and their idols led him away from pure worship of the true and living God. At the end of his life he seems to be bitter and nihilistic concerning the plight of man and what life is all about. While this doesn't take away from his writings, which many live by today from scripture or his contributions in the building of the magnificent Temple of Solomon, his moral failures did keep him from fullness in God. And his kingdom was divided, and his temple was eventually completely torn down.

I believe many of their issues and failures have been shown and openly revealed in scripture and the history books, for the last generation to have an example to enable them to make a greater commitment to stand against and resist the sexual immorality associated with this spirit of Jezebel. Their example should cause us to pursue the power of God available to us at the end of the age to stand against this spirit and tendency of sexual immorality of God's prophets. Paul tells us in 1 Corinthians 10:5 how God uses examples of good and bad from past generations to empower us to live different now in the present.

1Co 10:5 But with many of them God was not well pleased: for they were overthrown in the wilderness. 6 Now these things were our examples, to the intent we should not lust after evil things, as they also lusted. 7 Neither be ye idolaters, as were some of them; as it is written, the people sat down to eat and drink, and rose up to play.

8 Neither let us commit fornication, as some of them committed, and fell in one day three and twenty thousand. 9 Neither let us tempt Christ, as some of them also tempted, and were destroyed of serpents. 10 Neither murmur ye, as some of them also murmured, and were destroyed of the destroyer.

11 Now all these things happened unto them for ensamples: and they are written for our admonition, upon whom the ends of the world are come. 12 Wherefore let him that thinks he stands take heed lest he fall.

13 There hath no temptation taken you but such as is common to man: but God is faithful, who will not suffer you to be tempted above that ye are able; but will with the temptation also make a way to escape, that ye may be able to bear it. 14 Wherefore, my dearly beloved, flee from idolatry. 15 I speak as to wise men; judge ye what I say.

The Stand of Phinehas

If we're going to overcome the spirit of Jezebel at the end of the age we must learn from our past leaders successes and failures. If we're going to fulfill our end-time calling, it's going to require that this generation understand and take the purity stand of Phinehas. Phinehas was the Son of Eleazar, the high priest (Exo_6:25) of Israel, and he first comes on this scene in biblical history in Numbers 25. Phinehas' name means - Mouth of brass, or from old Egypt and is called, THE NEGRO. Phinehas was born from the marriage of Eleazar the son of Aaron to the daughters of Putiel. Putiel is an Egyptian name which means afflicted by God, which probably was derived from their time in Egypt (Africa) where they were in 400 years of bondage and slavery to the Egyptians.

While yet a youth Phinehas distinguished himself at Shittim by his zeal against the immorality into which the Moabites had tempted the people (Num_25:1-9), and thus "stayed the plague" that had broken out among the people, and by which twenty- four thousand of them perished.

Num 25:1 And Israel abode in Shittim, and the people began to commit whoredom with the daughters of Moab. 2 And they called the people unto the sacrifices of their gods: and the people did eat, and bowed down to their gods. 3 And Israel joined himself unto Baalpeor: and the anger of the LORD was kindled against Israel. 4 And the LORD said unto Moses, Take all the heads of the people, and hang them up before the LORD against the sun, that the fierce anger of the LORD may be turned away from Israel.

5 And Moses said unto the judges of Israel, Slay ye everyone his men that were joined unto Baalpeor. 6 And, behold, one of the children of Israel came and brought unto his brethren a Midianitish woman in the sight of Moses, and in the sight of all the congregation of the children of Israel, who were weeping before the door of the tabernacle of the congregation.

7 And when Phinehas, the son of Eleazar, the son of Aaron the priest, saw it, he rose up from among the congregation, and took a javelin in his hand; 8 And he went after the man of Israel into the tent, and thrust both of them through, the man of Israel, and the woman through her belly. So the plague was stayed from the children of Israel.

Here it is seen the pathway to purity and an everlasting priesthood. Phinehas takes a leading part in cleansing Israel from whoredom at Shittim. He there punished the brazen licentiousness of Zimri, prince of Sirecon, by slaying both him and the Midianite woman he had brought into camp. This incident is referred to in Psa_106:30, Psa_106:31. Then

Overcoming the spirit of Jezebel

stood up Phinehas, and executed judgment: and so the plague was stayed. 31 And that was counted unto him for righteousness unto all generations for evermore. For his faithfulness on that occasion he received the divine approbation (Num_25:10-13).

Num 25:10 And the LORD spake unto Moses, saying, 11 Phinehas, the son of Eleazar, the son of Aaron the priest, hath turned my wrath away from the children of Israel, while he was zealous for my sake among them, that I consumed not the children of Israel in my jealousy, 12 Wherefore say, Behold, I give unto him my covenant of peace; 13 And he shall have it, and his seed after him, even the covenant of an everlasting priesthood; because he was zealous for his God, and made an atonement for the children of Israel.

He afterwards commanded the army that went out against the Midianites (Num_31:6-8). When representatives of the people were sent to expostulate with the two and a half tribes who, just after crossing Jordan, built an altar and departed without giving any explanation, Phinehas was their leader, and addressed them in the words recorded in Jos_22:16-20. Their explanation follows. This great altar was intended to be in all ages only a witness that they still formed a part of Israel. Phinehas was afterwards the chief adviser in the war with the Benjamites. He is commemorated in Psa_106:30, Psa_106:31.

The Stand of Phinehas against Immorality and Sexual Perversion

In order to overcome the spirit of Jezebel and enter into a priesthood that is continued as an everlasting priesthood, not only must you come into maturity by the perfecting of the saints by the five-fold ministry gifts but you must stand against all idols and false gods of immorality and sexual perversion. Like Phinehas we need to be zealous for the honor of God being manifested in the midst of his people, while making atonement for the people through intercessory prayer. As Phinehas, while just a young man, was zealous for his God, interceding for God's honor, taking a stand against all immorality and false altars built over and against the altar of God, even so this end-time generation needs young men who will be zealous for God's honor amongst his people and stand against all immorality and imitations of God in this generation.

What was said of Phinehas must be said of the generation that enters through Jesus Christ into the everlasting priesthood after the order of Melchizedek - and that was counted unto him for righteousness unto all generations. Because of Phinehas' zealousness and stand against immorality he was given righteousness and a covenant of peace that would be everlasting, enduring throughout all generations after him.

The Results of the Reversed Curse of Balaam

The raising up of Phinehas to stand against the immorality of the children of Israel with the daughters of the Moabites was a direct result of the blessing of God released upon the children of Israel when Balak tried to get Balaam to Curse Israel. God wouldn't let him curse his people, reversing the curse and releasing the blessing. Two chapters later Phinehas rose up to deal with the iniquity and perverseness that was released in lieu of the curse. Balaam ended up blessing Israel when he was being paid and offered honor and fame to curse Israel. Phinehas was God's answer to Balaam's second option of causing Israel to be disqualified from the blessing through sexual immorality and perverseness. Num 23:13 And Balak said unto him, Come, I pray thee, with me unto another place, from whence thou mayest see them: thou shalt see but the utmost part of them, and shalt not see them all: and curse me them from thence.

Num 23:18 And he took up his parable, and said, Rise up, Balak, and hear; hearken unto me, thou son of Zippor: 19 God is not a man, that he should lie; neither the son of man, that he should repent: hath he said, and shall he not do it? or hath he spoken, and shall he not make it good? Num 3:20 Behold, I have received commandment to bless: and he hath blessed; and I cannot reverse it. 21 He hath not beheld iniquity in Jacob, neither hath he seen perverseness in Israel: the LORD his God is with him, and the shout of a king is among them.

Balak was trying to get Balaam to curse the children of Israel to keep them from travelling through their land on their way to their promise land. When Balaam was unable to curse the children of Israel, he told Balak, the Lord hath not beheld iniquity in Jacob, neither has he seen perverseness in Israel: the Lord his God is with him, and the shout of a king is among them.

Overcoming the spirit of Jezebel

Balak's aim after he had seen that Balaam could not curse the children of Israel was to cause the children of Israel to be disqualified through perverseness and immorality. But because of the God of righteousness that was among them they were not seen as perverse but as their God was righteous, so they were seen as righteous. Seeing yourself as God sees you is the first step out of immorality and perverseness. It's is not the aim of God's righteousness to overlook immorality, it is the aim of God's righteousness for his people to be delivered from immorality so that they might enter into an everlasting priesthood. What is keeping this generation out of their purpose and destiny in God? I believe it is the climate of immorality that is prevalent, not only in society, but also in the church at large of this generation. If we're going to enter into our priestly ministry we are going to have to resist all teachings and false grace messages that enable us in immorality in the church of this generation. Phinehas was raised up as a young man that was not influenced by neither his climate nor the false message of grace within the camp of Israel to take a stand against the message and the resulting acts of immorality within the camp. In Numbers 25 he was said to be zealous for His God and rose up from among the congregation and took his javelin in his hand and thrust them both the man from Israel and the Midianitish woman through their belly.

Num 25:6 And, behold, one of the children of Israel came and brought unto his brethren a Midianitish woman in the sight of Moses, and in the sight of all the congregation of the children of Israel, who were weeping before the door of the tabernacle of the congregation. 7 And when Phinehas, the son of Eleazar, the son of Aaron the priest, saw it, he rose up from among the congregation, and took a javelin in his hand; 8. And he went after the man of Israel into the tent, and thrust both of them through, the man of Israel, and the woman through her belly. So the plague was stayed from the children of Israel.

The Javelin through the Belly of Compromise Purifies Sexual Impurity

God is looking for young men that will rise up and be zealous for God, not being influenced by the climate of the false identity of stereo-typical sexuality in a gender or race, nor by the false grace message in the church of this generation, taking their javelin in their hand and thrusting it through the belly of the body of Christ that is compromising with immorality. Why did Phinehas drive the javelin through the belly? Why not the heart? Why not the temples in the head like Jael, Heber's wife did when she took a nail of the tent and drove it through the temples of Sisera in Judges 4:21? What does the belly represent? The Belly is the part of the body where life flows from. It's the part of the body where new life is birthed from. It represents fruitfulness. John 7:37, 38 says of the belly, that it releases living water from the body of Christ. This not only represents words of life spoken from the word of God, but it also represents the intimacy of relations that results when the semen is released from a man to a woman to produce life.

John 7:37 In the last day, that great day of the feast, Jesus stood and cried, saying, If any man thirst, let him come unto me, and drink. 38 He that believeth on me, as the scripture hath said, out of his belly shall flow rivers of living water. 39 (But this spake he of the Spirit, which they that believe on him should receive: for the Holy Ghost was not yet given; because that Jesus was not yet glorified.)

The Coming Youth Movement of Sexual Purity & Peace

The javelin through the belly of men, or through the compromising body of Christ signifies the stopping of the plague of sin. It signifies the stopping of the consequences of lack of true intimacy which is, barrenness, poverty, sickness and spiritual death. It will be stayed by the end-time Phinehas generation that will be raised up to initiate true intimacy and an everlasting priesthood, and covenant of peace to the end-time generation. This generation needs purity initiators. Men that will rise up out of a pure life and preach and teach against sexual immorality. This generation needs young men that will not compromise with sin and lead a generation of young men out of the bed of the sexual revolution that began in the 60's with the hippie movement. It is this purity and movement of purity that's going to release upon this generation the Covenant of Peace of Phinehas. What is this covenant of peace that flows from and is synonymous with this everlasting priesthood of Phinehas?

The Covenant of Peace

Num 25:12.13 Wherefore say, Behold, I give unto him my covenant of peace: 13 And he shall have it, and his seed after him, even the covenant of an everlasting priesthood; because he was zealous for his God, and made an atonement for the children of Israel.

God wants to give this generation the zealousness of Phinehas that turns His wrath away from the people of God. The covenant of peace that will be released to establish this everlasting priesthood within the body of Christ will consist of SHALOM; which is a spirit that releases;

1) *Completeness, soundness, welfare, peace a) completeness (in number) b) safety, soundness (in body) c) welfare, health, prosperity d) peace, quiet, tranquillity, contentment e) peace, friendship 1) of human relationships 2) with God especially in covenant relationships) peace from war.*

In order for this generation to enter into the Covenant of peace of this everlasting priesthood where we have completeness, safety, reconciliation, health, and prosperity, we're going to have to deal with the stereotypical thought patterns and cycles that are synonymous with our families that produce this climate of compromise and immorality that is anti- covenant.

The Jews are an example of a people of the Covenant.

The Jews are a people that hold fast to the covenant of their forefathers. And even though this covenant was cut over four thousand years ago it has taken them through many atrocities. Even though this covenant is now known in the bible as the Old Covenant, they still, as a people, are leaders in their communities, the moneylenders, the bank owners, the builders, the television and radio owners, the business leaders. With the keeping of the Old covenant alone they are the wealthiest people in our communities. They have the lowest prison population, below 1 percent, the lowest rate of divorce in their marriages, the lowest number of single parent homes. They are consistently seen in the upper strata of our society because they understand and hold to covenant relationships.

This anti-covenant climate in our churches can be attributed to our messages we are hearing in our Churches. We're going to have to deal with these messages that are being taught in our churches that produce this climate of compromise and immorality that are anti-covenant. Jesus addresses this spirit in the church by first addressing the doctrine that produced this spirit in the Church of Pergamos in the book of the Revelation.

The Doctrine of Balaam – The Producing of a Climate of Immorality

14 But I have a few things against you, because you have there those who hold the doctrine of Balaam, who taught Balak to put a stumbling block before the children of Israel, to eat things sacrificed to idols, and to commit sexual immorality. 15 Thus you also have those who hold the doctrine of the Nicolaitans, which thing I hate. (Rev. 2:14-15)

I have a few things against you – the two groups (Balaamites and Nicolaitans) were similar yet distinct. They both taught a perversion of the doctrine of liberty. They taught that it was okay to participate in the "partying and immorality" of that day under the pretense of Christian liberty.
4 Certain men have crept in unnoticed, who long ago were marked out for this condemnation, ungodly men, who turn the grace of our God into lewdness... (Jude 4)

Antinomianism is the belief that the Gospel frees us from obedience to specific moral standards since we believe that salvation is given as a gift by faith, therefore, we do not need to repent. [Greek: anti-nomos (law)]. You have there those who hold the doctrine of Balaam – the doctrine of Balaam involved participating in temple feasts and their orgies. Some of the leaders in the church taught it was okay to participate in these parties or pagan feasts.

Who taught Balak to put a stumbling block before Israel, to eat things sacrificed to idols, and to commit sexual immorality – Balaam advised King Balak to defeat the Israelites by getting them to participate in feasts related to idolatry and immorality (Num. 25). This caused God to judge Israel. The Israelites came under God's judgment as 24,000 people died. A stumbling block is a trap that when triggered, shuts on its prey.

This refers to anything which causes a person to fall into sin. You also have those who hold the doctrine of the Nicolaitans, which thing I hate – this refers to followers of Nicolas, the Jerusalem deacon who fell into error (Acts 6:5). This was the common view among the early church Fathers. For example, Irenaeus in the second century taught that the Nicolaitans were without restraint in their indulgence of the flesh, especially with immorality. This distortion of "liberty in grace" that allows for compromise with a sinful culture, is prevalent in the church today. This view best represents what Jesus was saying in this passage. This doctrine and practice was also prominent in Ephesus (Rev. 2:6).

6 But this you have, that you hate the deeds of the Nicolaitans, which I also hate. (Rev. 2:6)

Twice Jesus mentions His hatred of the Nicolaitans. What were deeds in Ephesus were doctrines in Pergamos. The teaching allowed the spirit of compromise to go unchallenged. The church continued to allow those who held the teaching of Balaam and the Nicolaitans. They had not purged themselves of such as the church in Ephesus did (Rev. 2:6).
The Spirit of Jezebel.

Taking the Stand of Phinehas

In order to take the stand of Phinehas to establish purity and an everlasting priesthood there is three specific areas we must take stands in.
1. We must stand as a friend of the bridegroom –John 3:29
2. We must stand as a prophetic voice with the whole armor of God on - Ephesians 6:12, Jeremiah 23:18
3. We must stand against sexual immorality – Psalm 106:19

Standing as a Friend of the Bridegroom

Joh 3:29 He that hath the bride is the bridegroom: but the friend of the bridegroom, which standeth and heareth him, rejoiceth greatly because of the bridegroom's voice: this my joy therefore is fulfilled. 30 He must increase, but I must decrease.

The Greek word for "Friend" is philos (fee'-los) which means, properly dear, that is, a friend; actively fond, that is, friendly (still as a noun, an associate, neighbor, etc.): - friend. To be a friend of the bridegroom is to be dear to him and him to you, to be fond of him, to be an associate or a neighbor, or to live and work near him. A friend of the bridegroom is one that is in an intimate relationship with the Lord Jesus Christ, where we love him with all our heart, mind, soul and strength, and where we choose his love over the love and pleasures of this life.

The Outstanding Characteristics of the Friend of the Bridegroom

According John 3:29-31 there are 4 particular points of a friend of the bridegroom that will cause us to stand as Phinehas did zealous for the honor of the Lord

1. That he loves to hear the bridegroom's voice. He rejoices greatly in hearing his voice.

2. He stands in continual covenant, abides with the bridegroom through thick and thin, no matter what comes.

3. The friend's joy is fulfilled when the bridegroom is being heard.

4. The friend decreases so that the bridegrooms influence and effect can increase.

CHAPTER 13

THE NEW HEART RELEASES YOU FROM THE JEZEBEL SPIRIT

> Ezekiel 36:26 *A new heart also will I give you, and a new spirit will put within you: and I will take away the stony heart out of your flesh, and I will give you a heart of flesh, and I will put my spirit within you, and cause you to walk in my statues, and ye shall keep my judgments, and do them.*

The Bible says in I John 4:8 that *God is love.* Therefore to truly love or to know how to love we must know the love of God, and know the love that God has for us. This is where we see the problem in society today, where the love of many has waxed cold. We don't know God, nor do we truly know the love God has for us. Therefore we have left the first commandment - our Love with all our hearts for God. As a result we have lost, misplaced and replaced Love for one another for lust, motivated by the spirit of Jezebel, in this harlot Babylonian system.

Jesus defined loving God as being deeply rooted in a spirit of obedience (Jn. 14:15, 21, 23; Deut. 6:1-9). There is no such thing as loving God without seeking to obey His Word.

15 "If you love Me, keep My commandments..." *(Jn. 14:15)*

To encounter God's love in significant ways we must recognize the small insignificant ways He loves us. God's love is manifested by the keeping of His commandments. However, the good news is that these commandments from the Law of Moses, known as the 10 commandments, are fulfilled by Jesus. In Jesus all the commandments of Moses are fulfilled in two. Exodus 20 tells us what the commandments of Moses are.

Exodus 20:3
(1) Thou shalt have no other gods before me.

(2) *4. Thou shalt not make unto thee any graven image,* or any likeness of anything that is in heaven above, or that is in the earth beneath, or that is in the water under the earth: 5. Thou shalt not bow down thyself to them, nor serve them: for I the LORD thy God am a jealous God, visiting the iniquity of the fathers upon the children unto the third and fourth generation of them that hate me; 6. And shewing mercy unto thousands of them that love me, and keep my commandments.

(3) *7. Thou shalt not take the name of the LORD thy God in vain;* for the LORD will not hold him guiltless that taketh his name in vain.

(4) *8. Remember the Sabbath day, to keep it holy.* 9 Six days shalt thou labor, and do all thy work: 10 But the seventh day is the Sabbath of the LORD thy God: in it thou shalt not do any work, thou, nor thy son, nor thy daughter, thy manservant, nor thy maidservant, nor thy cattle, nor thy stranger that is within thy gates: 11 For in six days the LORD made heaven and earth, the sea, and all that in them is, and rested the seventh day: wherefore the LORD blessed the Sabbath day, and hallowed it.

(5) *12. Honor thy father and thy mother:* that thy days may be long upon the land which the LORD thy God giveth thee.

(6) *13. Thou shalt not kill.*

(7) *14. Thou shalt not commit adultery.*

(8) *15. Thou shalt not steal.*

(9) *16. Thou shalt not bear false witness against thy neighbor.*

(10) *17. Thou shalt not covet thy neighbor's* house, thou shalt not covet thy neighbor's wife, nor his manservant, nor his maidservant, nor his ox, nor his ass, nor any thing that is thy neighbor's.

Jesus sums up these 10 in Matthew 22:37, in response to a question from a lawyer that came to him saying;

36 Master, which is the great commandment in the law? 37 Jesus said unto him, Thou shalt love the Lord thy God with all thy heart, and with all thy soul, and with all thy mind. 38 This is the first and great commandment. 39 And the second is like unto it, Thou shalt love thy neighbor as thyself. 40 On these two commandments hang all the law and the prophets.

Within the 10 commandments there is the commandment forbidding the sexual sin of Adultery, which is sex outside of the context of marriage between a man and a woman. Jesus addresses and confirms this in Matthew 19:4-9 saying;

4 And he answered and said unto them, Have ye not read, that he which made them at the beginning made them male and female, 5 And said, For this cause shall a man leave father and mother, and shall cleave to his wife: and they twain shall be one flesh? 6 Wherefore they are no more twain, but one flesh. What therefore God hath joined together, let not man put asunder. 7 They say unto him, why did Moses then command to give a writing of divorcement, and to put her away? 8 He says unto them, Moses because of the hardness of your hearts suffered you to put away your wives: but from the beginning it was not so. 9 And I say unto you, whosoever shall put away his wife, except it be for fornication, and shall marry another, commits adultery: and whoso marries her which is put away doth commit adultery.

Any sexual act outside of the context of the marriage between one woman to one man, is forbidden in the Law of Moses, and according to Jesus, to love God we must keep His commandments. We must love God on his terms, not on our own terms. Many attempt to love God on our terms without keeping His commands or without obedience to Him. Again, the good news is that Jesus kept the commandments and fulfilled them all, in his life, death, burial and resurrection, releasing the grace for us to walk in the power of his finished work of righteousness.

True love can only be found in God and a heart that has been cleansed and forgiven of sins by the blood of Jesus. Our society has replaced God's love and traded it in for the lust of this world. We have given up on God's love and given in to lust and immorality and have called it love, but this so-called love actually leads to the ways of death and destruction. Matthew 24:10 *says because iniquity shall abound, the love of many shall wax cold.* The lack of true love always comes about from the lack of a heart after God. The lack of God's love and the lack of a heart after God always comes from a hardened, stony heart.

What is God's Love

The Spirit's first agenda is to establish the first commandment in first place in the Church (Mt. 22:37-38). Because of how He feels about us, He wants us to respond to Him with all our love. He created us in His likeness with a capacity to participate in this fellowship of the burning heart. God's very own love is imparted to His people by the Holy Spirit (Rom. 5:5). We love Him because He first loved us (1 Jn. 4:19). We are empowered to love by first receiving His love. God's Love can be seen in all of its fullness by the act of Him sending His Son to die on Calvary. The Cross is the epitome of the Love of God expressed to mankind. Until we get a revelation of the Cross and all it represents to us of the Love of God we will not have the ability to experience God's love in our emotions.

32. He that spared not his own Son, but delivered him up for us all, how shall he not with him also freely give us all things? (Rom 8:32)

9 In this was manifested the love of God toward us, because that God sent his only begotten Son into the world, that we might live through him. (1Jn 4:9)

The New Heart and Sexual Perversion

We need a new heart that will transform us from a sinful, stony heart to a heart of flesh. God wants to give us this new heart to deliver us from the stony heart that causes us to go after our own sinful, lustful desires. When we get a New Heart we will turn from sexual perversion, we will turn for sexual sins, and we will turn from the false gods of Jezebel. God wants to take us away from this stony heart and give us this heart of flesh.

> Ezekiel 36:26 *I will take away the stony heart out of your flesh, and give you a heart of flesh.*

If we understand what the stony heart is, along with the heart of flesh, we will then know what the new heart is. Is the heart of flesh an organ or a person? Is the stony heart an organ or the condition that his people had ended up in?

Mans Need for a Heart Transplant

Man was created in the image of God, meant to reflect the glory of God in the earth. But because of sin, man fell from grace and fell short of the glory of God. Unable to reflect the glory of God, man began to reflect the nature of the god of this world. Man began to operate out of the spirit of this world, which is the lust of the flesh, the lust of the eye, and the pride of life, which are all three, anti-covenant, and anti-relationship. No longer able to operate out of the heart of God, he began operating out of his sin-filled heart. Man's heart with all of its characteristics was meant to mirror the heart of God. As God's heart is comprised of 12 dimensions, man's heart was to be comprised of the same twelve dimensions so that man could feel what God feels and relate with one another as God relates with us.

However, with the fall of man and the decline of his heart to the ways of the wicked one, man began to lose touch with how God feels and how God relates with humanity and began to relate with God and one another how Satan relates with God, separated from Him and in rebellion to Him, attempting to be like God in the earth without God. God created us to be like Him, through fellowship, submission, and relationship with Him. But after Adam and Eve's rebellion we became disconnected with God and out of touch with his nature and his heart. And so for the last 6000 years, since the fall of man in the garden, man has been living out of his sin-filled heart. The sin-filled heart of man is comprised of these 12 dimensions as found in scripture.

1. **A Wicked Heart**- Prov. 10:20; 26:23 *the tongue of the just is as choice silver: the heart of the wicked is little worth. Burning lips and a wicked heart are like potsherd covered with silver dross.* The word wicked means to be twisted. This type of heart makes us twisted in our sinful nature. This means that we are unable to see straight, and understand things the way they were meant to be. Therefore we end up doing things that have twisted what God originally meant them to be.

2   **An Evil Heart**- Gen. 6:5 *And God saw that the wickedness of man was great in the earth, and that every imagination of the thoughts of his heart was only evil continually.* This type of heart causes man to have vain, twisted imaginations. When a man's thoughts are twisted and un-productive his heart and actions are going to be also. Man's evil heart comes from what he thinks about most of the time. And what he thinks about most of the time comes from having received a warped view of life, an unbelieving world view. The evil heart also deals with unbelief. Heb 3:12 says *Take heed, brethren, lest there be in any of you an evil heart of unbelief, in departing from the living God.*

3   **A Deceitful Heart**- Jer. 17:9 *the heart is deceitful above all things, and desperately wicked: who can know it?* This type of heart makes us lie and deceive to obtain. Once we allow our focus of life to get off of God and get it on the twisted system and nature of this evil world we then find ourselves trying to get what God intends for us to have in him through the arm of the flesh, and our own deceitful way. Because we are unable to receive those things as a result of sin that does not negate the fact that we yet still have a God-given desire for them. When that God-given desire meets our inabilities and shortcomings of sin we then find ourselves lying and deceiving to obtain what we see and desire to have.

4   **A Proud Heart** - Psa.101:5 Prov. 21:4;28:25 *Whoso privily slanders his neighbor him will I cut off: him that hath a high look and a proud heart will I not suffer. A high look, and a proud heart, and the plowing of the wicked, is sin.* This type of heart makes us not want to listen to others. This type of heart makes us feel as if we are the highest of the highest and no one knows more or should know more than us. A person with a proud heart has a hard time receiving or listening to anyone. Therefore any one that might be a threat to their position in their mind they will slander or reveal their shortcomings. This is all to put themselves up higher in the eyes of others.

5   **A Froward Heart** - Psalm 101:4 Prov11:20; 17:20 *A froward heart shall depart from me: I will not know a wicked person. They that are of a froward heart are abomination to the Lord. He that hath a*

froward heart finds no good. The word froward means to be crooked. This type of heart makes us crooked. It makes us not want to walk circumspectly. When a person has a froward heart they often are thinking of many ways to get over on someone. They are always thinking of ways to cause their will and desires to be done at the expense of another.

6 **A Perverse Heart** - Prov. 12:7-8; 23:33 *A man shall be commended according to his wisdom: but he that is of a perverse heart shall be despised.* The word perverse means to willfully look to make the right wrong and the wrong right. It is a calculated, planned effort and attempt to cause what is known to be the wrong thing, wrong way, or wrong path to be accepted as the right. This is what we see happening is our society today.

7 **An Impenitent Heart** - Rom. 2:5 *But after thy hardness and impenitent heart treasures up unto thyself wrath against the day of wrath and revelation of the righteous judgment of God*: To have an Impenitent heart is a little different than having a hardened heart. It is to be unwilling to repent for a wrong. Or to be unrepentant. When you receive an Impenitent heart you know you need to change but you decide not to. A hardened heart is refusing to change because of a pattern that has been developed causing one to feel as if they can't change so they refuse to try.

8 **A Foolish Heart** - Rom. 1:21 *Because that, when they knew God, they glorified him not as God, neither were thankful; but became vain in their imaginations, and their foolish heart was darkened.* To be without understanding and knowledge willfully. To say there is no God even though all the evidence points to the fact that there is. This heart makes a person refuse knowledge and understanding that they know to be truth.

9 **A Gross Heart** - Matt 13:15 *For the people's heart is waxed gross, and their ears are dull of hearing, lest at any time they should see with their eyes, and hear with their ears, and should understand with their heart, and should be converted.* This is a heart of one that has ears dull of hearing, and eyes that are closed. This is a heart that has become gross, meaning that their spirit is blinded and

unable to see or hear because of the darkness of life that one lives in.

10 **A Rebellious Heart** - Jer. 5:23, 24 *But this people hath a revolting and a rebellious heart; they are revolting and gone.* This type of heart is a heart that does not respect authority. They do not fear or respect God or anyone else. There is no fear of God in their hearts. They refuse to submit to anyone.

11 **A Double Heart** – I Chronicles 12:33 *Of Zebulun, such as went forth to battle, expert in war, with all instruments of war, fifty thousand, which could keep rank: they were not of double heart.* This type of heart is a heart that's unsure about what place and position they are to fill. So they jump in and out of responsibilities, commitments, assignments, and covenants. This type of heart is unable to commit to one thing, they go back and forth from one thing to another, from one position to another, from one person to another, and from one job to another. Always trying to do something else that they were not ordained, or anointed to do.

12 **A Stony/Hardened Heart**- Ezekiel 32:26 Hebrews. 3:8; 4:1-7 *Harden not your hearts, as in the provocation, in the day of temptation in the wilderness:* this type of heart makes us refuse to change, refuse to submit and refuse to obey. It was this type of heart in the children of Israel that caused them to come short of what God had promised them. Because of a hardened heart they wandered in the wilderness for 40 years until they all died. When we end up with a hardened heart it is as a result of seeing and hearing the right way but refusing to change because of what we are used to, or because the change is more difficult than we expected.

These are the 12 dimensions found in the bible of the heart of sinful man. Genesis 6 tells us that as a result of sin man's heart became desperately wicked. It became man's nature to be sinful, to be vain in our imaginations, to be deceitful, to lie, to refuse change, to be crooked, to be prideful. All of these characteristics of man's evil heart are anti-relational. With the characteristics of man's heart being of such, it became evident, around the time of Noah's generation in Genesis 6, that man was on a relational collision course towards destruction and if there was not a change then man would destroy his environment and himself. It so repented God that he had made man that he decided to end the entire world and every one that had become victims of that environment and begin again with Noah, a righteous man that had found grace in the eyes of God. A man with the heart of God will always be a man that is righteous (in right standing) with God and man in relationships. Thusly, returning to the heart of God always results in being returned to right relationship with God and man through the grace of God.

> Genesis 6:8 But *Noah Found grace in the eyes of the LORD. These are the generations of Noah: Noah was a just man and perfect in his generations, and Noah walked with God.*

The stony heart actually represents the Ten Commandments, written upon tables of stone, which was the heart of their relationship with him in the Old Covenant. The heart of children of Israel's relationship with God was Laws written upon stone. This, because they were flesh and blood, caused their response to a God that they could not see, except on stones, to be hardhearted and stiff-necked. Their hearts became like the very stones that the laws were written upon. Because they could not see him, touch him, or feel him, they had a hard time obeying him. God was saying to the children of Israel in Ezekiel 36, I will take away the foundation and center of your relationship with me, which are the Ten Commandments on tablets of stone, and I will give you a person, Yeshua, which will be the *New Heart*, or center of your relationship with me. And then you SHALL Love me with all your heart, mind, soul and strength. The heart of flesh would then represent a person, Yeshua, the incarnate word, being the center of their relationship, communion and fellowship with him, not the commandments written upon stone.

Jesus is the New Heart that God gave them. The heart is in the center of the body, and is what pumps blood throughout the body. The heart is the source of your relationship with all the other organs in your body. Symbolically speaking the heart, your feelings, will, and emotions are the source of your covenant relationships with your covenant partners. It is the lifeline of all of your relationships. When God said I will give you a new heart he was saying, I will give you a new center or source of relationship with me and with your fellowman. He was saying, I will give you a new mediator, a new intercessor, a new bridge between me and you and between you and one another, not the stony heart, or center of the 10 commandments but the fulfillment of those commandment - Jesus the Christ.

The Holy Ghost, the New Spirit

As Jesus is the New Heart, the Holy Ghost is the new spirit that he put within them. Notice he gave them a new heart but he put within them a new spirit, because God gave his Son to reconcile the world unto himself. But his son sent the Holy Ghost to live in us to empower us to be witnesses of him. It would be the new spirit that would empower them to live out everything their relationship with Jesus would reveal to them. It would be the New Spirit that would energize and give life to the new heart.

It would be the new spirit that would cause them to walk in the statutes of Jesus, keep His judgments, and do them. This would cause them to dwell in the land that he gave their fathers; and be called his people and he be their God.

Once the God nature within is restored we can be completely delivered from the focus on the desires to fulfil the lust of the flesh. We lust of after the desires of the flesh mainly because we are living after and under the spirit of the world. According to the scripture in 1 John 2:16. It states;

For all that is in the world—the lusts of the flesh and the lusts of the eyes and Pride of Life—is not from the Father (God) but is from the world. 17 And the world is passing away along with its desires, but whoever does the will of God abides forever.

Once we realize the God nature within us, and all that he has for us, we will return to the place of our original sprit led, spirit dominated focus after the heart of God.

Acts 13:22 And when he had removed him, he raised up unto them David to be their king: to whom he gave testimony, and said, I have found David the son of Jesse, a man after mine own heart, which shall fulfill all of my will.

The Heart of God assures you of doing all of the will of God for your life. God can't release wealth unto you until He imparts His heart into you. David was a man of great wealth who passed that wealth on to his son Solomon. Solomon became the wealthiest man in history, because God personally testified of David, "I have found David the son of Jesse, a man after mine own heart, which shall fulfill all My will." When we receive the heart of God, we qualify for all He has, of which we need to accomplish the will of God in the earth. This includes money, wealth, and riches.

What is the Heart of God? The Twelve Dimensions of the Heart of God

It is not until our hearts are made new that we will be able return to the right relationships with God and man necessary to possess great wealth. Man's sin filled heart it made it impossible for man to keep covenant with God or one another. Thus, because of sin, man is in need of a restored heart. Man is in need of a heart transplant. In the beginning, when Adam and Eve fell, man's heart became separated from the heart of God; thus, causing man to also be separated from the will of God.

God said in Ezekiel 36:26:

A new heart also will I give you, and a new spirit will I put within you: and I will take away the stony heart out of your flesh, and will give you a heart of flesh. And I will put my spirit within you, and cause you to walk in my statutes, and you shall keep my judgments, and do them.

Through much prayer, study, and investigation of the Word of God on the subject of the heart of God, I have found that there are 12 dimensions to the heart of God that lead us from our sin filled heart to the new heart. God reveals all of them in His Word. When our hearts are transformed by the power of God and we are given the new heart, we are delivered from the Jezebel spirit and given power over all sexual perversion and every work of demonic power in the earth. The number 12 in biblical numerology represents governmental order in the

Kingdom of God. There were the 12 tribes of Israel. There were the 12 Disciples. There are the 12 gates of the city. There are the 12 stones in the foundation of the city. 12 is twice the number 6, which is the number of man. The first man Adam was created on the 6th day, making 6 the number of man. Jesus is referred to as the last Adam, and as man's physical heart is made up of six components the spiritual heart from God is comprised of 12 distinct characteristics or dimensions.

All of these 12 dimensions of the heart of God were seen in the life of Jesus, the last Adam, and deal with an aspect of man's ability to enter into and remain in covenant relationship with God and man. In this chapter, we will briefly discuss all 12 characteristics of God's heart so that we can be restored and experience complete, full, uninhibited relationship with God and our fellow man.

The 12 dimensions of the Heart of God with their definitions are:

1. A Clean Heart – Psalm 51:10; John 13:10, 11 Loyalty in covenant relationships
2. A Pure Heart – Matthew 5-8 Right motives in covenant relationships
3. A Perfect Heart – 1 Chronicles 12:38 Purpose, position, and rank in covenant relationships
4. An Upright Heart - Psalm 7:10, 32:11, 36:10, 97:11 Integrity and trust in covenant relationships
5. A Tender Heart - 2 Kings 22:19 Submission, yielding, and forgiveness in covenant relationships
6. A Prudent/Wise Heart - Proverbs 18:15 Discernment, wisdom and right choices in covenant relationships.
7. A Willing/Free Heart - Exodus 35:5 Sacrificial giving in covenant relationships.
8. A Merry Heart - Prov. 15:13; 17:22 – Joy and healing in covenant **relationships**
9. A True Heart - Hebrews 10:22 - Openness, candidness and truthfulness in covenant relationships
10. An Understanding Heart- Psalm 49:3 Intimate knowledge of seasons, times and ways in covenant relationships.
11. A Good and Honest Heart- Luke 8:15/Matthew 12:35 Patience and fruitfulness in covenant relationships.

12. A New Heart - THE HEART OF GOD Ezekiel 36:26 The keeping of standards commitments, commandments, and statutes in covenant relationships.

In defining these 12 facets of the heart of God and contrasting them with the aspects of man's sin filled heart there is one singular common thread that runs through all twelve: COVENANT RELATIONSHIPS. We need not look any further than what sin has done to distort man's relational capabilities towards his God and with one another to understand why we need a heart transplant.

God is a relational God. God is a God of covenant. The very essence of His nature is rooted in his ability and desire for covenant relationship with his subjects. Sin distorts and diffuses relationships with God and man. In the beginning, sin separated man from the heart of God and man's heart became incapable of having fruitful, productive relationships.

Covenant relationships are what God is all about and covenant relationships are what man was created to live by. It was covenant relationships with God and man that sin destroyed, and it was covenant relationships with God and man the Jesus came to restore.

Therefore if any man be in Christ, he is a new creature: old things are passed away; behold all things are become new. And all things are of God, who hath reconciled us to himself by Jesus Christ, and hath given to us the ministry of reconciliation; To wit, God was in Christ, reconciling the world unto himself, not imputing their trespasses unto them; and hath committed unto us the word of reconciliation. Now then we are ambassadors for Christ, as though God did beseech you by us; we pray you in Christ's stead, be reconciled to God. For he hath made him to be sin; that we might be made the righteousness of God in him. 2 Corinthians 5:17-21

Covenant relationships flourish where righteousness is exalted, and covenant relationships deteriorate where sin abounds. Matt 24:12 says: And because iniquity shall abound, the love of many shall wax cold. Therefore it is covenant relationships that the new heart heals and restores. It is when our hearts are made new by the spirit of God that we are once again capable of having and maintaining quality, prosperous, covenant relationships. Ezekiel 36:26 and Jeremiah 31:31-33 bears this out.

These two verses sound similar. However, the emphasis of one is a new heart and the emphasis of the other is a new covenant.

A new heart also will I give you, and a new spirit will I put within you: and I will take away the stony heart out of your flesh, and I will give you a heart of flesh. And I will put my spirit within you, and cause you to walk in my statutes, and ye shall keep my judgments, and do them. Ezekiel 36:26, 27

Behold the days come, saith the Lord, that I will make a new covenant with the house of Israel and with the house of Judah: Not according to the covenant that I made with their fathers in the day that I took them by the hand to bring them out of the land of Egypt; which covenant they broke, although I was a husband unto them saith the Lord; But this shall be the covenant that I will make with the house of Israel; After those days, saith the Lord, I will put my law in their inward parts, and write it in their hearts; and will be their God, and they shall be my people. Jeremiah 31:31-33

Ezekiel 36 speaks of God's people receiving a new heart so that they might be capable of walking in the statutes and judgments that were synonymous with their covenant. Jeremiah 31 speaks of a new covenant that would be established with the House of Israel that would entail them having the laws, the judgments and statutes written on their hearts and not just their minds.

The laws, commandments, statutes and judgments of the Old Testament were the covenant requirements and stipulations for the children of Israel. Every covenant has these requirements and stipulations as a part of the covenant contract. These stipulations from God were a part of their contract in their covenant with God. They were to keep these as a binding contract that was not to be broken. However, this new covenant that Ezekiel speaks of was going to have these laws, commandments, statutes and judgments written on their hearts, not just on a piece a stone, so they could keep these laws naturally, as a part of their righteousness nature.

Therefore, one scripture in Ezekiel speaks of a new heart, and the other in Jeremiah speaks of a new covenant. One speaks of a heart to keep the covenant, and the other speaks of a covenant to change and keep their hearts.

The Two Covenants

There are two main covenants the Bible is founded upon: the Old Covenant and the New Covenant. One was the covenant the Children of Israel would try to keep with their evil heart; the other covenant was the covenant that all men could keep because of their new heart. One, the Old covenant, was a covenant that would reveal and make known man's evil heart, and the other, the New Covenant, was the covenant that would reveal and make possible the new heart.

What is a covenant? A covenant is a binding agreement or promise of blessing, provision and protection between two or more parties. It is an agreement between two parties; a binding, solemn vow; a corporate resolution. It literally means to come together. It is a mutual understanding between two parties, each binding to the other to fulfill certain obligations. I believe this is something we have lost in our generation, both in the church of our generation and secular world. We have lost the meaning and significance of what a covenant is, as well as the power and seriousness of a covenant. The church needs to rediscover what a covenant is and begin to clearly understand the power of covenant in the Word of God. When we realize what has been afforded us in the blood covenant, we wil be revolutionized in our relationships with both God and man. We also will never again settle for anything less than what Jesus died to give us: our healing, deliverance, money, prosperity, household salvation, the earth and all that is therein.

When we rediscover what covenant is in the church the world will have a model to see to establish the meaning and power of covenant relationships. When this happens, we will see the foundations of our existence, which is marriage, family and community, restored, and blessing, favor, and wealth will once again abound in the earth.

The church however, must rediscover the meaning and seriousness of covenant if the world is ever going to be restored to its value. In the church, covenant relationships have become secondary to religious practices. Covenant is not the emphasis; religion and religious practices have been the emphasis. To have knowledge of the scriptures and knowledge of salvation without revelation knowledge of the blood covenant is to make the Word of God concerning salvation and all that salvation entails, of none effect in the life of the believer. Salvation is not a religious act received on the basis of our works; it is a covenant act freely given by the blood of Jesus.

If the New Testament Church really had a handle on the covenant, we would have already possessed the wealth of the wicked; instead of just talking about it. If we really had a handle on the covenant we would have already become the head and not the tail in the earth, not just confessing it. If the New Testament church had a handle on covenant we would already be walking in divine health and wealth, not just believing for healing and prosperity. Any people that get an understanding of covenant, and value its' function and operation benefit from its blessing and are naturally raised to the forefront and pinnacle of life and living.

The Jews and Their Covenant Understanding

The Jews are an example. They are a people that hold fast to the covenant of their forefathers. Even though this covenant was cut over four thousand years ago, it has taken them through many atrocities. Even though this covenant is now known in the Christian Bible as the Old Covenant, they still, as a people, are leaders in their communities: the moneylenders, bank owners, builders, television and radio owners, and business leaders. With the keeping of the Old covenant alone, they are the wealthiest people in our communities. They have the lowest prison population, the lowest rate of divorce, and the lowest number of single parent homes. They are consistently seen in the upper strata of our society because they understand and hold to the covenant of their fathers. Therefore, they are able to forge, build, and remain in covenant relationships in their families and with their fellow man.

As Christians with the Old and New Covenant, we are still living beneath our privileges and not seeing the full blessings of God as we should. Our homes break up at the same rate as that the secular world's homes do. Our children end up in jail at the same rate that the unchurched. We are in as much debt and financial lack as the unchurched. Our credit rating is no better, and sometimes worse than the un-churched. Why is this? It is because we have embraced the religious ideology and philosophy of Christianity, but have not embraced an understanding of what it means to be in a covenant relationship. Therefore, we wear the tag without the items. We have the name without the blessing. We carry the banner without the victory.

If we understood covenant, both old and new, and walked in a true covenant relationship with God and man, there are no words that could express the magnitude and enormity of the blessing that the church would receive in the earth. A Christian with the Old and New Covenant should be blessed beyond that of the wealthiest Jew with just the Old covenant. There is no measure or barometer that could keep track of our status and position in the earth. There would be nothing we could compare to what we would be manifesting and walking in in this life. It hasn't been seen yet. Isaiah 64:4 says: For since the beginning of the world men have not heard, nor perceived by the ear. Neither hath the eye seen, O God, beside thee, what he hath prepared for him that waits for him. (The NT in 1 Corinthians 2:9, the things that God hath prepared for them that love him.)

Without an understanding of covenant, beginning with the Old Covenant, and without the heart of God to fulfill our end of the covenant with God, the church will continue to talk of the blessings while others that know the value of covenant possess those blessings. The church will continue to confess and believe God is a healer without ever possessing the faith to see that healing manifest in this life. The church will continue to confess and believe that they are the head and not the tail while continuing to be second class citizens subject to the world. The church will continue to confess and believe that they are the lenders and not the borrower while continuing to borrow money to buy their cars, and build their houses and churches.

The God nature that has to be restored within us is the heart of God: the nature of covenant relational capabilities to God and man. Once we see this covenant nature restored within us, we will see complete deliverance from sexual perversion and total power to once and for all overcome the spirit of Jezebel.

OTHER BOOKS BY BRONDON MATHIS

The 12 Dimensions of the Heart of God- 12 Steps to Becoming a Person or Church after God's Own Heart -

As we move further into the second decade of the 21st century there's a sense that the second coming of Christ is nigh at hand. As His appearing nears the Spirit of God is prompting men and women in prayer rooms and houses of prayer all over the world to go from seeking God for material things and shallow spiritual experiences to seeking, like David, after One Thing - The Beauty of God's Heart - To behold the beauty of the Lord. In this book Brondon Mathis gives revelation on the 12 dimensions of what's on God's Beautiful Heart for His church and His people at the end of the age, to raise up a people who will fulfill all of the will of God for their generation. It describes each characteristic of God's heart in detail and will take the reader on a 12-step journey from their own heart to God's own Heart.

List Price: $14.99

Overcoming the spirit of Jezebel

My Home shall be called the house of Prayer - Our Family Vision for training our children in the way they should go.

List Price: $14.99

The Church without Spot or Wrinkle - 7 steps to Becoming A Pure & Spotless Bride Ready For the Day of the Lord -

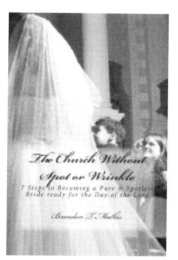

The Church without Spot or Wrinkle reveals how the end-time Church will be prepared as a bride adorned for her husband, right before the coming Day of the Lord, by taking heed to the messages given to the seven churches of Asia in the book of the Revelation.

List Price: $14.99

My House shall be called the House of Prayer. The 7 Principles to becoming a Praying Church -

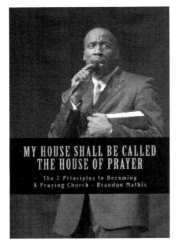

Mat 21:13-16 And He said unto them, (It is written), My house shall be called the house of prayer (for all nations); but ye have made it a den of thieves. From these verses in Matthew 21:12-18 there are 7 principles, all of them beginning with a "P" that will return the end-time church back to her calling as the house of prayer. This book is aimed at exploring these 7 principles for the purpose of restoring joyful prayer back to the church of the 21st century, to enable her to fulfill her end-time mission in the earth of preparing the way for the coming of the Lord

List Price: $14.99

The Coming FORERUNNER Ministry Out of AFRICA - Africa & African America's End-Time Calling bringing Gods house of Prayer to Reconciliation and Fullness -

At the end of the age God is releasing His spirit to prophetically call forth a unique group of end-time forerunners out of Africa & the African Diaspora to arise, shine with light in the time of gross darkness, to take their place of leadership in the earth, to stand shoulder to shoulder with the nations of the world to lead the church to reconciliation and fullness. **List Price: $14.99**

The Melchizedek Priesthood of Jesus Christ - *The 7 Steps to The Priesthood of The Believer in God's House of Prayer* -

There are many functions of ministry that Jesus undertook while on the earth. He operated as an Apostle, he operated as a Prophet, as a Pastor, he operated as a Teacher and as an Evangelists. However, of all those ministry offices the greatest ministry function that Jesus operated in while in the earth, and the ministry that he still functions in while seated at the right hand of the father, is the ministry office of a High Priest, after the order of Melchizedek. He is an intercessor, ever living to make intercession for His people to be reconciled to God. This ministry of reconciliation from the priesthood of Melchizedek is the main ministry that Jesus came to fulfill. **List Price: $14.99**

My Money is Restored - **Preparing To Arise During The Coming Financial Fall Out** -

All indicators say our economic system in America and the world is headed for a complete financial collapse. If we act now to free ourselves from this debtor system and learn how to operate with godly wisdom and discipline with our resources, we will not only survive this coming economic disaster, we will ARISE AND THRIVE and see the long awaited transfer of the wealth of the nations into the hands of the righteous. "MY MONEY IS RESTORED" will explore the life of the biblical personality Joseph in Egypt, along with His principles for money restoration, and unconventional strategies for accumulating wealth during down economic times in the world's financial markets. My Money is Restored is aimed at empowering believers to operate within the world's financial markets, through unconventional wisdom, by the system and principles of the Kingdom of God, to establish wealth and financial abundance during times of lack, for the preservation and glorification of the Church in the earth. **List Price: $14.99**

Upon This Rock I will Build My Church -The End-Time Purpose of the Church built upon the book of the revelation

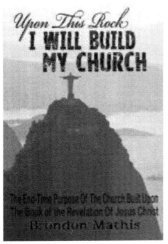

From Matt 16:13-17 this book will explore the Rock that the church was built upon to position her to accomplish her end-time purpose in the earth. From these verses we can see clearly what the rock is. #1 The Church was built upon the Revelation of Jesus Christ - Thou art the Christ, the Son of the Living God. #2 The Church was built for battle - the gates of hell will not prevail against it. #3 The Church was built upon Prayer, to bind the kingdom of darkness, and to release heaven on earth - and whatever you bind on earth shall be bound in heaven... whatever you loose on earth will be loosed in heaven. To accomplish her mission the church must understand the person revealed in the book of the Revelation of Jesus Christ. Only the church built upon this rock will be able to withstand the gates of Hell at the end of the age, to prepare the earth for Jesus' return.

List Price: $14.99

Building Cities of Refuge – **Preparing cities through 24/7 Worship & Prayer for the Coming Systemic Collapse –**

"Building Cities of Refuge" is a book on how certain cities will be positioned during the unique dynamics surrounding a coming systemic collapse to thrive, not just survive, during the most difficult times in all of Human History. This book reveals that by as early as 2015, because of this coming systemic collapse, the Church in our nation is going to need to develop relational networking communities and regions of economic and agricultural supply for our livelihood, to be able to survive, as well as thrive during these times. These communities will be called CITIES OF REFUGE & POCKETS OF MERCY. God is moving on believers in these designated Cities of Refuge, all over the nation and world, to begin building City Churches for 24/7 day and night worship and prayer, along with storehouses for storing food in these communities; places where people can come and receive spiritual and natural food and essentials for living during this coming systemic collapse. This book will present some of these solutions and scriptural paradigms for cities of refuge, as well as wisdom and principles for living for the Church during this time.

List Price: $14.99

The Beginning of Sorrows – *Biblical Paradigms for the comfort and peace of Jerusalem in Times of Conflict*

As the Peace talks between Israel and the Palestinian Authority continue to produce little results, and while a nuclear Iran becomes a reality right before our eyes, Jerusalem is coming upon a season that Jesus prophesied about in Matthew 24:8 called the Beginning of Sorrows. What should be our response to this season of conflict and impending war in Jerusalem and the Middle-East? Where should believers in Christ stand on the issue of Jerusalem and how should we pray? In this book, the Beginning of Sorrows, Brondon Mathis shares from a divine encounter he had in the city of Jerusalem, which unlocked for him the biblical text of Matthew 24, that is meant to position Jerusalem to be prepared for this season of sorrow, as well as for the return of her Messiah, who will ultimately bring an end and peace to this ancient biblical conflict.

List Price: $14.99

In the Beginning of Sorrows you will learn:
1. What really is the Peace of Jerusalem?
2. What one sign from Matthew 24 will initiate the Beginning of Sorrows in Jerusalem?
3. How will God comfort Jerusalem with His rod and staff?
4. What are the coming Judgments of the Four Blood Moons?
5. What is the gospel that must be preached before the end to this conflict comes?
6. How do we correctly pray for the Peace of Jerusalem?
7. How will All Israel be saved from the desolation of this Holy City?

Brondon Mathis is an ordained ministry of 28 years, having served on the staff and leadership team of the International House of Prayer in Kansas City, as well as 8 years on the Pastoral Staff at World Harvest Church in Columbus Ohio. While on staff at World Harvest Church he was director of Evangelism and Outreach, establishing & operating its inner city ministries called Metro Harvest Church. Comprised of four Satellite Community Centers on each side of town, these centers, called Hope Centers, were established by Brondon Mathis to minister to thousands in the inner-city of Columbus Ohio. Over a 5 year period over 10,000 souls were saved and discipled from the government projects of the inner cities through His ministry. Brondon Mathis is committed to seeing the Church returned to her covenant roots, as well as the release of Justice in the inner-cities of the earth, through day and night prayer, the performing arts, and feeding ministries to the poor. He is married to Noe Mathis and they have 5 children.

Contact info:
Brondon Mathis
614-949-2474, office
614-745-9683, cell
yeshuamovement@gmail.com
www.yeshualifecenter.com
facebook/brondonmathis.com

Made in the USA
Lexington, KY
05 May 2017